The Anxiety Expert

A Psychiatrist's Story of Panic

by

Marjorie Raskin

authorHOUSE

AuthorHouse™
1663 Liberty Drive
Bloomington, IN 47403
www.authorhouse.com
Phone: 833-262-8899

This book is a work of non-fiction. Unless otherwise noted, the author and the publisher make no explicit guarantees as to the accuracy of the information contained in this book and in some cases, names of people and places have been altered to protect their privacy.

Published by AuthorHouse 08/24/2020

ISBN: 978-1-4184-2668-2 (sc)
ISBN: 978-1-4184-2669-9 (e)

Library of Congress Control Number: 2004096500

Print information available on the last page.

Any people depicted in stock imagery provided by Getty Images are models, and such images are being used for illustrative purposes only. Certain stock imagery © Getty Images.

The author gratefully acknowledges permission to reprint lyrics from THE MOTORCY-CLE SONG By Arlo Guthrie © Copyright 1967 (renewed), 1968 (renewed) by APPLESEED MUSIC, Inc. All rights reserved. Used by permission. And lyrics, page 8, from 'This is The Army, Mr. Jones by Irving Berlin © Copyright 1942 © Copyright renewed © Copyright Assigned to Winthrop Rutherford, Jr., Anne Phipps Sidamon-Eristoff and Theodore R. Jackson as Trustees of the God Bless America Fund. International Copyright Secured   All Right Reserved   Reprinted by Permission"

This book is printed on acid-free paper.

For Keith, Ali, and Fred
All My Love

ACKNOWLEDGEMENTS

I want to thank
Myra Goldberg, who started me off by believing in this venture.
Kathleen Hill, one of the kindest individuals I have ever known,
who patiently and for many years, helped shaped my book.
Barbara Probst Solomon, who with humor and savvy offered
excellent advice.
My writing group — Barbara Bonn, Karen Regen, Nancy
Somerfeld, and Maureen Pilkington — who read, corrected, reread,
and still smiled.
Alexis Raskin, Keith Raskin, and Kim Su Theiler, who offered
encouragement, advice, and sharp nudges at key times.
Fred Greenleaf, my husband, who did the brunt of the editing,
listening, and essential hand holding.

"It wasn't the height; but the distance. It was his vast, lonely distance from everyone who mattered."

The Accidental Tourist by Anne Tyler

Chapter 1. I Fall Up

On the morning of my forty-eighth birthday I sat in bed picturing the endless Monday meetings, the pink phone slips piling in my box, the eager psychiatric residents each with impossible questions. It was a typical Monday morning — ordinarily I'd have seen the kids off, gulped down my coffee and been rushing out the door — but that morning I felt oddly not myself and called in sick.

I leaned against my pillow, my mind hopping from worry to worry — had I mailed the Con Ed bill? Should I reconnect my smoke alarm? Did I need a stronger front door lock? Sick of my thoughts, I walked to the living room and for a distraction picked up Anne Tyler's *Dinner at the Homesick Restaurant*. I went back to bed, pulled my blue comforter up to my chest, and lost myself reading.

I didn't realize it was after four until I heard a book-bag thud to the floor and my daughter in the kitchen.

"Happy Birthday," Alexis said, handing me a vase with four yellow roses. She curled beside me and talked about her day. Suddenly she bounced up and asked if I wanted to come shopping with her. I said yes, but when I started to get up, a lightness floated to my head. I rested until it passed, then hoisted myself on an elbow; the lightness came back. I stayed home, convincing myself I was simply tired, and I told myself the same thing when I wasn't up to going out for my own birthday dinner.

The next morning I headed out to Jefferson Market planning a feast for my kids. As I entered, I saw a woman who looked familiar. I smiled, but instead of smiling back, her eyes grew wary and deep grooves creased the sides of her mouth. As I watched she seemed to turn into a frightened old lady. I rushed to the meat counter. Standing there, looking through the glass at endless rows of chicken parts, my legs started to buckle. Afraid of falling to the floor, I clutched at the top of the counter. I was resting against it, taking deep breaths, when Richard, the manager, appeared.

"What's wrong, Doc? You want a chair? A glass of water?"

I forced myself to straighten up and smile. "Just getting over a flu," I said. "A weak moment."

Leaning on my cart, I turned quickly down an aisle and out of Richard's sight. Cans of Campbell's soup towered precariously above me on one side, and on the other I saw spires of spaghetti sauce in glass jars. I moved forward and stopped by the paper goods. *All right, your anxiety's back, but you've got to keep going! You've been through this plenty of times before! For godsake you run an anxiety clinic!*

Wednesday was even worse. Once outside, I clung to the powdery bark of a Gingko tree, watching taxis tear down the block, their drivers so intent, I felt they wouldn't notice if I fell right in front of them. I lurched back to my apartment and thought about what to do. Then I called an analyst I'd heard good things about. He sounded nice, but said he didn't have time until next week. When I explained I was a psychiatrist having trouble getting to work, he squeezed me in on Friday. That gave me a lift.

By Thursday morning I felt eager to take charge of my life again. I swallowed a Valium and waited for it to kick in. The room smelled of dirty socks; so did I. I took a shower, which I saw as a major achievement. I even blew my hair dry and put on bright red lipstick.

Opening my apartment door, I faced a six-foot hall of large black tiles. The air around me grew thin. My tongue swelled in my mouth. A vague nausea ticked at the back of my throat. As I thought about crossing the threshold, a voice in my head whispered *You'll fall. You'll scream. You'll act crazy!* But when I hesitated, another voice said *Quitter. Loser. Want to be stuck in that apartment forever?* I stood swaying on that threshold for what seemed like hours, my heart pounding into my brain.

I yanked the door closed and rested against it. This had to be a mistake. I was a doctor, an associate professor, a good mother who was there for her children. I could always fight my anxiety before, but this was different. Something inside me had sat down and was refusing to budge. I didn't know what that was, only that it was pressing me against some rock bottom place I'd barely even glimpsed before.

Despite my profession and many attempts at treatment, I'd never really looked at my own life.

Chapter 2. The House on Avenue L

First grade had just ended and I see myself outside P.S. 193 in the Flatbush section of Brooklyn. Along with the other children, I was leaping, shouting and shoving my fists into the hot June air. Then I crossed Bedford Avenue to reach my house, a solid white stucco that stood catty-corner to the school.

I went straight to my mother's room but her door was closed, which meant she was napping or doing whatever she did when she got back from teaching. I coughed a few times, and with Lucky trotting beside me, went to the breakfast room. Soon my mother came in, wearing her blue robe, one side of her hair flat against her head. She was a tall woman with deep-set brown eyes, creamy white skin and a Roman nose she claimed made her ugly.

"I had this big fight with Jerry," I said, sitting across from her.

"Why do you even talk to him? He only wants to hurt you." My mother patted her pockets, looking for a cigarette. The skin around her nails was red and ragged; tiny spots of color flashed off her enormous diamond ring.

Yollie, our housekeeper, brought tea in thin pink cups, then returned with a plate of Mandelbrot, the finger-sized cookies my mother liked for dunking.

"It's time you understood what people can do when they're jealous," my mother said, choosing a cookie. "Your father's an important lawyer. Mr. Silverman's what? — a butcher. I'm a bookkeeper who made herself into high school teacher while Mrs. Silverman, on her best days, can barely move dust from one spot to the other. And we're the only family on the block that can afford a live-in maid, but that's not why Jerry's really jealous."

My mother's strong white teeth bit through the cookie.

"Nope, he hates you because you're better than he is."

I gulped my tea, unable to believe my mother's words. Jerry lived three houses down, and even though we fought, we were always together. I reached down and scratched Lucky's thick white ruff. As my fingers moved into his fur, I sensed my mother's eyes on me, waiting for an answer.

"I won't ever let Jerry play with Lucky again."

"Why have anything to do with him at all? But first, go wash your hands."

When I came back, a curl of smoke was rising from the table, and my mother had that look she got whenever she thought about her own mother's death. I moved an ashtray under her hand; when she was like that, she'd just let the ashes fall off in clumps. She didn't look sad or happy, but intent like someone tuned to a radio station that barely came in.

My grandma Golda had lived with us and taken care of me. My mother said that was the happiest time of Golda's life, but that happiness was cut short by the brain tumor that killed her. Her death plunged my high spirited mother into a grief that lasted years.

At dinner that night, I looked up at my father and said, "School's over!"

"You must be happy," he answered, finishing his fruit cup.

I nodded, my eyes on his. I never did anything alone with him and wanted that to change. He was always busy, and my mother warned me not to disturb him. She said that since he worked for the city — for Mayor LaGuardia himself — not only did he have to read all the legal papers he carried home each night, but the newspapers too. Yet other fathers went out with their kids. I saw them.

I sat watching as my father cut his chicken.

"So, it's a big day for you," he said, the chicken still on his fork.

I nodded, not touching my own food.

He lay his fork on his plate. "Look, after dinner why don't we walk up to Nostrand and get an ice cream? Would you like that?"

Like it? I was ecstatic. After dinner he put his suit jacket on. He never went out without a tie and jacket. I pushed my blouse into my skirt and strode out beside him.

At first we walked in silence. After a few moments, I asked, "Do you ever see my report card? I get really good grades."

"And I'm making sure you can be anything you want without worrying about money the way I did." He drew a pack of Camels from his pocket and, tapping the bottom, made several cigarettes jump up. He lifted one out and held it with smooth curved fingers as he spoke. "I think doing what interests you is the most important thing in life. I love law — oh, not every single case, but the law itself, the reasoning that goes into making legal decisions."

"Maybe I'll be a lawyer too."

He brought the cigarette up to his mouth. "Why not, you've got a good head for logic." There was a yellow flash of light and his cigarette was lit.

My mother claimed that since I was a girl I had to be a teacher, or a librarian, or something else that got me home early. But here was my father opening a whole new world, just as easily as he'd lit his cigarette.

At the candy store on Nostrand, Mr. Weissen, the owner, was behind the counter. He was an angry old man with garlic pickle breath. Before going in, the kids would pinch their noses and fan their faces; sometime they did it inside too, which made Mr. Weissen yell for us to get out. I thought of that skinny old man as a joke, but when we walked in, my father nodded courteously and asked how business was.

Mr. Weissen shrugged his narrow shoulders.

"And Ralph," my father continued, "How's our Ralph?"

Mr. Weissen's crumpled face opened into the first smile I'd ever seen on him. He pointed to a picture tacked onto the back wall of a chunky young man with short blond hair under a sailor cap. My father leaned across the counter. "Such a fine young man," he said.

6

Mr. Weissen wrapped my cone with a napkin and handed it to me with a proud little flourish.

Walking back, I squinted up at the father I hardly knew. On Sundays other lawyers often came over to talk to him. I never thought much about it, but maybe he had a special way of making things work out. I pictured him sitting behind a big desk at City Hall, listening to the Mayor's problems and solving them. Yet, with all that on his mind, he still thought about me and my future. I licked my chocolate cone and edged closer to him.

I began the summer trying to stay away from Jerry as I'd promised. But since there was no one else our age on the block, he'd be waiting on my stoop each morning with comic books and bubble gum. In a couple of days, I let him come along when I threw balls to Lucky. Lucky was part sheltie, with long thick hair and small stand-up ears. Once he had the ball he'd run with it until I caught him, so this worked best when someone else headed him off. Soon things went back to normal — with Jerry, me and Lucky spending all our free time together.

"You're riding for a fall," my mother said after seeing me with Jerry. "The boy's vicious. Why don't you play with Laura next door, or that nice Ginsberg girl?"

"They're two years older, Ma. They don't want me hanging around."

"I told you I was the only Jew in my whole neighborhood. If I waited for invitations like you do, I'd have always been alone. You've got to learn to push yourself forward."

My mother picked up her silver mirror with the naked lady on the back, arched her chin, and plucked out two black hairs. She could push herself in ways I couldn't. On summer evenings she'd put on a scoop-necked dress, powder her nose, dab on pink lipstick, and sit in front of the house with the neighbors, laughing and telling her funny stories. She did that even on her worst days, days when she'd stayed inside, her blue robe on, following Yollie and talking about how unfair it was that a good woman like her mother was struck down just on the verge of living. Touching her large gold cross, Yollie would say, "Ain't much fairness to be found in this world." Sometimes those words calmed my mother, but at other times she'd go on about how Golda's speech got so jumbled at the end that people shunned her, and the headaches, and the operation where they sliced off the top of her head "like a soft-boiled egg." When she got to that point, she'd be curled up on the sofa weeping into her fists.

"Please, Mrs.Tucker," Yollie would say, "Don't upset yourself like this. Put on a pretty dress and go out for a bit. Come, I'll help you find something." Then Yollie, a big-headed woman not much taller than I was, would lift my long-limbed mother off the couch and guide her down the hall. At those moments I understood Yollie's importance. I wasn't even two when my grandmother died, so I didn't remember her. But I did remember my mother crying in bed for days, her door closed against me.

The summer went by quickly. Second grade started off with a play. We were well into World War II then and sang "This is the Army, Mr. Jones. No more private rooms or telephones." I had a big speaking part, and the teacher dressed me in a white oak tag bonnet, a blue blouse, and a long red crepe paper skirt that rustled as I walked. After the play, I wore the costume home so my parents could see it. When I charged through the door, Lucky wasn't there, so I called out, "Lucky, come on boy, come see me." Sometimes he was in back, so I called louder. Still no Lucky. Thinking he'd gone into the street, I started toward the front door. Yollie came after me, her flat face pale, her mouth open.

"Where's Lucky?"

"Your mother's on her way home right now. She'll tell you."

"Where's Lucky?" My voice was edging higher.

"You have to wait and hear it from your mother. That's how she wants it." Yollie's eyelids began twitching the way they did when she had a toothache.

I sank into a chair, tears rolling down my face.

"Do you want some tea? Some soda?"

"No. Nothing."

I didn't want Yollie to see me crying, but as she started down the hall, I discovered I didn't want to be alone either.

"Maybe I'll have some tea," I called after her.

She came back and actually looked worried about me. She fussed in the kitchen and brought out a big cup of sweet milky tea. I sat sipping it. Yollie stayed in the kitchen looking in on me from time to time. She had short arms and legs, and coarse brown hair that sprung from low on her forehead.

When I heard my mother's car, I jumped from my chair.

"Be strong, Margie," my mother yelled out, rushing toward me. "Lucky needs you to be strong now."

I felt myself breathe again. So Lucky wasn't dead. My mother sat beside me and took my hand. "Lucky's been drafted. The Army took him today. There's nothing I could do."

The newsreels were full of pictures of dogs at war, and I pictured Lucky running beside them wearing a little harness like they did. "Will he come back?" I asked.

"That's hard to say. He'll be trained to deliver messages, then he'll go to the front."

She sighed and looked into my eyes. "I think the best thing is for you to be brave, and pray. Ask God to watch over Lucky when he's on his missions."

Yollie who'd been listening, turned away and walked quickly down the hall. My mother pulled me against her, and rocked me, singing "*I lalul, I lalul, I lalula lalula* Margie." I relaxed in her arms.

Jerry met me on my stoop as usual after school. "I'm sure going to miss Lucky," he said.

"Well, he could come back."

"Come back? Are you crazy?"

"Not everyone in the Army gets killed, you know."

Jerry started laughing, belch like sounds shot from his mouth. "If he comes back, it'll be as a pancake."

"You're the crazy one." I stood up and looked for a stick to poke at Jerry's eyes. My mother was right; he was vicious.

"Look, I got sent home from school early yesterday. Lucky was in the gutter. There was a bloody towel over him, but I could still see where he was all squashed in the middle. Yollie was standing over him, holding her cross and crying. Now that's the truth!"

"No. It's not. You're only saying it because you're jealous."

"Jealous? Jealous of what?"

Jerry turned his face up, so I was looking into big round nostrils like in a pig's snout.

"Because. Because my father's an important lawyer and my mother's a teacher, and we have a live-in maid and lots of other things too."

"Jealous of you?" He snorted. "That's a hot one. Do you know what my mother tells me when I'm bad? That she'll send me to your house for a day. She says Yollie watches you so close you can't even flush until she looks."

I must have blushed or something, because Jerry's eyes gleamed with excitement, and he smacked his hands on his thighs. "If you don't go for a day, does she shove a hose up your tush?"

I jumped on Jerry, sinking my teeth into his shoulder and digging at his face with my nails. He must've been hitting me too, but I didn't feel it. I heard kids yelling and felt hands pulling at me. Yollie appeared, hands on her hips, and ordered me into the house. I ran past her and slammed my bedroom door in her face.

Jerry was talking about the most shameful secret of my life. It wasn't enemas, but slivers of soap that had the same effect, one that Yollie stood watching. Just lying on my bed, I felt sick. I tried to keep those memories away, but they paraded before me. I dug my nails into my palms, but still they taunted.

I lay on the bed for a long time before I felt the mattress sag as my mother sat down. "Of course Lucky's alive," she was saying. "We should be hearing about him soon. They promised to call." She leaned over and moved my bangs against my forehead. "I love you," she said. "I love you more than life itself."

While my mother was talking, I was remembering other things I didn't want to think about. Ever since I could remember, Yollie had been on some mission to control me. Before the stuff in the bathroom, she talked about black spots on my soul and locked me in the coal bin in the cellar whenever I didn't obey her fast enough. She'd stand outside the bin door — wooden with gaps at the top and bottom — and talk about a green and yellow monster who lived there and ate children. Then she'd go upstairs, leaving me in a dark stall that smelled of scummy water, afraid every time I heard a noise that the monster was coming.

The first time it happened, I ran and told my mother. "But Yollie loves you," she said. "She'd never do anything to hurt you." When it happened again, I ran back to her. "Yollie loves you," she repeated, her eyes filling with a sadness too heavy for her. I backed off and never said anything about it again. But that day, with those memories, love was not a word I wanted to hear from my mother.

While we were walking on Nostrand the next evening, my father said, "I'm sorry about Lucky. I miss the little guy myself."

"What happened to him? Tell me the truth."

"The army took him just like your mother said." He plucked the stem of a privet bush and rolled it with his fingers. He was upset but he still seemed solid, so I felt better.

"Do you think he'll come back?"

My father touched my shoulder. "Even soldiers aren't coming back. If I were you, Margie, I wouldn't count on it."

That was hard, but I knew that sometimes one person had to say hard things to someone else. I walked for a while thinking, all right, your mother has her problems, but at least your father's strong.

"Did you know that Yollie used to lock me in the cellar?" I heard myself say.

My father stopped and turned to me. "No, I never heard anything like that."

"Well, she did." Anger was rising up inside me, but it wasn't Yollie I was angry at. It was my mother. I wanted him to know how she took care of me.

He took his glasses off, huffed onto each lens, and polished them with a big white handkerchief. "I'll look into it. Then we'll talk again." He walked slower after that, and he looked different — caved in, older. I turned my head away.

The next night when we got ice cream, my father was quiet. He never did say anything about Yollie and the cellar, that night or any other. At first I was so angry, I didn't want to go anyplace with him again. Then I figured my mother said it didn't happen, so of course he believed her.

The next morning, Jerry was outside my house. "I'm sorry. I mouthed off too much," he said. He put his foot on the bottom step. "Who told you Lucky was in the army?"

"My mother."

Jerry nodded, pulled a piece of brown paper from his pocket and smoothed it in his hand. It was a diagram that showed my house on the corner of L and Bedford and two big X's. "Here's where Lucky got hit. There was blood on the street." He pointed to one X. "And here's where Yollie stood over him." He pointed to the other X.

"You're crazy," I said, but my words had no bite.

He looked straight at me, his pale eyes blinking. "Lucky was run over. Parents shouldn't lie to their kids." Jerry handed me the paper and wandered off. I rumpled it in my hand, lifted my arm to throw it after him, then slipped it in my pocket.

That Sunday we were going to a birthday party for Beaty, my father's youngest sister. These parties were important to my mother who'd been cooking and shopping for days. I was upset about Lucky but still I wanted to go.

I slipped into the plaid dress my mother had laid out. In the living room, I sat waiting while she rummaged in the cellar for platters, and my father showered. I heard a crash and looked outside to see a car with its front bumper locked to the back of ours. I hollered for my mother as the car surged forward, lurching from side to side. Finally it broke free and headed down Bedford Avenue. Our car inched forward, then stopped.

When I told my mother what happened, she bent and looked out the window.

"Our car's exactly where I parked it. I remember how far it was from the hydrant."

"But I saw it," I argued. "I saw that car hit ours."

"No, it's exactly where I parked it. It's got to be all right. We're using it today. "

I lay my head against the back of the couch and watched her open the hall closet and slip her arms into the sleeves of her black Persian lamb coat. She took down a matching cap and fussed with it until one dark curl lay flat against her cheek.

Suddenly, I pictured myself, rock in hand, smashing her head to a pulp. My heart started racing, perspiration streamed down my back, and I sat forward, staring at my hands. That one image of me attacking my mother frightened me more than anything that had ever happened with Yollie. I sat frozen until my father came in.

"A car hit ours," I said. "I saw it."

My mother slid one gloved hand through my father's arm, and guided him toward the door. "Don't worry Oscar. You know Margie and her imagination."

Following them out, I felt so stiff it was hard to put one foot in front of the other. My mother climbed in front with her packages. I dragged myself in behind her. My father walked around the car, eyeing it closely. A spark of hope shot up inside me. When he turned the key, our car sputtered and died. My hope shot higher. He turned it again and the car started. But we only got a few feet before there was a crash and the sound of metal dragging. We jumped out to see our back bumper hanging off. I felt triumphant, thinking now my father would believe me about the car and Yollie. Why, any minute now he would sweep me up in his arms, kiss me on the cheek, and beg my forgiveness. And I would give it. Of course I would.

My father crouched in back of the car, moving the bumper up and down.

"Will we be able to drive it there?" my mother asked.

"Only if I can get this reattached."

As he headed to our garage my father avoided my eyes. That's when I knew how things stood.

"I'm not going with you!" I shouted. "I'm not going anyplace with you ever again. You're just like she is — a liar who believes only what you want to."

I ran across the lawn heading to the front of the house.

"Wait," my mother called after me.

"Let her be," my father said.

I went to my room and sat at my big maple desk, thinking that I was strong, certainly stronger than my parents. And I thought about Lucky too. He was dead and I felt like crying, but wouldn't give into it. I had to be beyond tears, beyond believing people I couldn't trust, beyond needing anyone but me.

My parents never did get to the party. Sometime later my father walked to my door and knocked. "Are you okay?" he called softly.

"I'm fine," I snapped. "Just fine."

Chapter 3. A Salvation of Sorts

At twelve I had two best friends, Harriet and Ann. Harriet had fine features, light brown hair, thin lips and braces. Ann was darker, fuller featured with soft down on her upper lip. After school we went to each other's houses, fixed each other's hair, and talked. We talked about love, sex, and the big question — when to go All The Way.

Harriet had a consistent answer. "After you're married."

Ann waffled. "When you're engaged. Well, if it's really love."

And I, three-time reader of *The Amboy Dukes* and twenty-eight time reader of the page where the girl in the car yells she's got to have it, would think, and sometimes say, "You do it when you want to."

Ann and Harriet looked at each other and laughed. I didn't mind; I was afraid of boys, and everyone knew it. When the spinning bottle pointed at me, I'd rush off to the bathroom. I thought Harriet and Ann were afraid of boys too. I believed most women were afraid of men, or the men were afraid of women. I didn't know which was true, but I was sure something like that went on.

Sometimes when my parent's friends came over, my mother would tell joke after joke about sex, like the one about the boy who, after seeing a woman's hairy armpits, exclaimed, "Goody, goody, two more places!" When she went on like that, my father would tighten the knot on his tie, close his jacket and sink further back in his chair. My mother would watch him out of the corner of her eye.

Suddenly she'd smile triumphantly, and change the subject. I didn't know what that was about, but it made me squirm and feel closer to my father.

I liked going to school and being out with Harriet and Ann, but when I walked through my front door, a sadness often came over me. Sometimes it got so bad I'd burst out crying at the table. My father would draw his eyebrows together in a look of concern, while my mother would lay her fork across the edge of her plate and say, "What now?" in a hoarse voice.

This time I cried harder.

"Did something happen at school? Did someone say something to you?

"NOOOOOO."

"Are you sick? Does something hurt?"

"NOOOOOO."

"Then why are you crying like this? You have everything. Everything! You're healthy, bright, nice looking. What's God going to think to see you, a girl with EVERYTHING, crying like this? He'll give you something to cry about. That's what He'll do."

Without looking up, I knew her lips were pale and her eyes bulging. A jealous vindictive God, the God that took my grandmother, seemed to hover above us. Like two leaves on a winter branch, my mother and I trembled in unison until my father said, "Come on Lily, stop it."

My mother took a breath, and told me to go wash my face.

When I came back, Yollie was clearing the dishes slowly, one by one. She looked much older with her hair smoothed back and parted in the middle. Her lips formed an encouraging smile, but I looked away. My crying jags seemed to have triggered her warmth.

At lunch one day Yollie sat across from me, a cup of black coffee in her hand, her expression open and expectant. I wanted to talk about myself, but not with her. I squinted at the yellow poppies that bloomed forever on that wallpaper. She rested her elbow on the table, took a long sip of coffee, and studied my face.

"You know, the best way to fight hate is with love," Yollie said.

I looked up, then quickly back down. *Hate? I hated her, but there was good reason for that. And yes, sometimes I got angry with my mother, but I kept that anger down, worked not to show it. What was she talking about?*

Yollie smiled and fingered her cross, which looked so heavy and solid. "You're not alone in your struggle. God watches you all the time. If he sees you want to change, He'll help. With Him on your side you can't lose."

On my side? That God who wants to punish me just for crying?

"You're struggling. I see it every day. But there's a way out. His love is enormous. Let it feed yours."

I walked away, thinking Yollie's off on one of her tangents.

Before I was thirteen, Yollie went back to Scranton to care for her sisters and brothers; her mother was sick. I never found out why she did those things when I was younger, but I think it was some kind of religious zeal, maybe the way she was raised. But I didn't think about her then. I wanted her gone, out of my life — forgotten.

Yet after she left I'd lie in bed at night thinking about the things she'd said. My mother was tired when she got home from work; she'd sit on the sofa, stretching her neck from side to side. I'd go up behind her and place my hands on her shoulders. It was hard to touch her; the first time I did it, it surprised me how hard it was. But that was good, the greater the struggle, the more it counted. I rubbed the knobs at the top of her spine until she sighed and let her head loll forward. When my fingers moved under her hairline, dandruff fell on my hands. I wanted to pull away, but didn't. Later, I'd sit on my father's footstool and ask about his day. When I first did that he'd looked surprised, but I kept asking until he told me work was nerve-racking. LaGuardia was sick and decided not to run again. He told my father that because he was a Jew he couldn't go higher but could be demoted. My father joined a private firm and said that was a whole new world. He'd cough nervously, and I'd sit willing his tension into my body.

I was working to be a saint, but every time I started feeling pleased with my progress, something inside my head rang with laughter, said *—You're such a fraud. How can you stand yourself?*

In my room I sat on my bed staring at its high, round posts, thinking hard about my life. I was frightened by things inside me that I didn't like or understand. My mother had a friend, Sally, who came over often to show us her new black mink coat, diamond stud earrings, cultured pearl necklace, or red silk dress. While she whirled around, her eyes begged us to adore her, yet no matter what we said her eyes stayed empty. I could be just like her: I could pamper myself endlessly and I'd always want more. But there was another way. I could lose myself in the unquestionably good.

I'd thought about being a doctor on and off for years. My aunt Beaty wanted to be one, but because polio made her walk with crutches, medical schools turned her down. She became a bacteriologist instead, and from her, I heard stories of medical discoveries. How she and others threw out bacterial cultures killed by an annoying mold until Fleming, realizing the mold's importance, discovered penicillin. My mother who worried she had this or that, saw Dr. Goldberg often and came back happy. Every October, I came down with bronchial pneumonia and Dr. Goldberg would cure me. One Sulfa tablet and I felt better. It amazed me. It felt like magic.

Sitting on my bed that day, I decided I'd be a doctor. Then people would be eager to see me, my phone would ring off the hook, my own mother would ask me questions and be pleased with my answers. I'd put polio on a slide and look at it so hard, it would yield up its secrets. Yes, medicine was the answer. After deciding to be a doctor, I didn't cry at dinner anymore. I ate quickly so I could get back to my room to study. I always studied a lot, but after that I studied methodically, and I stopped watching the way the popular girls arched their backs and looked up through their lashes when they talked to the boys. Boys didn't interest me anymore. I had a higher calling.

"You have a choice of high schools," my mother said when I was thirteen, sitting beside me on our green velvet sofa. Since Avenue L was the dividing line between Midwood and Madison, I could give an address across the street and go to Midwood. Midwood was the newer school; the richer, more popular kids went there. I'd just as soon go to Madison, I told her. Harriet and Ann would be there too.

"Well, Madison's a fine school." She slipped off her navy pumps and pressed her toes against the coffee table. I was surprised she wasn't fighting me more; I knew most of her friends' children went to Midwood.

"Madison's actually better for me," I confided. "I don't want to be bothered with all that social stuff. I have to study to be a doctor."

My mother smiled. "Didn't you want to be a Vet last year, right after Sparkles had her kittens? And what about being an artist? Why am I driving you for painting lessons every Tuesday?"

"I've changed. I know exactly what I want now."

"You're so silly. Only girls who don't marry become doctors. You'll marry. Why, you get prettier every day. You're going to be a knockout — what with your father's face and my body." Tall and elegant in her navy skirt and jewel neck blouse, my mother walked to the mirror in stocking feet, cupped her hand over the end of her nose, and still laughing, turned her head from side to side. Her dark hair swung out. "See, you'll look like this, only prettier."

"But I want to be a doctor because I have to be one. That's all I want."

"Why are you so afraid? Is it because you're so flat still? They'll grow. You've got my body, and I'm well over a B cup." She opened her jacket and cupped her breasts.

Embarrassed, I turned my head away. My mother laughed and laughed, and suddenly her laugh became a cackle. I turned to see if that sound was coming from her.

"My average is 97.4," I said, handing her my report card in the middle of my freshman year of high school.

"By mouth or rectum?" she cackled.

"An average is critical for getting into Medical School." My tone was huffy, superior. I was stepping into a world she couldn't know or understand. She taught only commercial subjects like bookkeeping and typing.

"Listen." My mother walked over and stood beside me, her face tilting down. "I'd gladly trade 20 of your I.Q. points for a normal daughter, a daughter with friends and dates. I kept my mother's house so lively she didn't have time to worry about her problems. But what do I get from you? Nothing. You don't bring friends home because you can't make them."

"I can too. I have friends — Harriet and Ann. I walk to school with them every day."

"Sure. And your blouse never hangs out of your skirt. And those food spots I can't see on the edge of your blouse — are they from today or last week? And your hair looks terrific hanging down against your face."

I watched my mother's thin red lips moving over her strong white teeth. That mouth came closer. "Just tell me one thing. Are you doing this to spite me?"

"No, of course not. *" You're nothing to me. You're not important enough to spite.*

"Good, because you're only hurting yourself. Medical Schools are like colleges. They want popular students with all kinds of interests."

I felt gutted, hollow as a chicken the butcher held up for my mother's approval. I looked down at the spots on the edge of my blouse, the dirty whites of my saddle shoes, the long threads sprouting lushly from my socks. *I'd never be a doctor. I'd never be anything.*

"Please don't look like that!" My mother lifted my face with long white fingers. "I'm sorry. Sometimes my mouth runs off with my head. I love you. You know that."

I nodded. She did love me. She just wanted me to be more like her friends' kids. I wanted to be more like them too, but couldn't. I was halfway to my room when she called to me.

"You know what we should do right now? We should go to Lupu's and buy you some nice clothes. That's my whole point. You don't have to look like this. You can be popular too."

The large back room at Lupu's had a mirror covering one wall. In my white slip, I hid behind a narrow curtain. My mother burst in, a pile of clothes over one arm. She unbuttoned a maroon dress with a Peter Pan collar. At her command, I walked back and forth across the room, bent, stretched, stood before the mirror. She knelt behind me, pulling the dress tight against my waist in front. "I can make darts right here. You see what that does?" I did see. And it thrilled me to have a figure.

As we walked to the car carrying our shopping bags, my mother sang, *"Ich bin die keinig foon dem yom"* — "I am the captain of the sea." She'd become the business manager of a Hadassah group that put on Gilbert and Sullivan in Yiddish and sent money to Israel. Evenings and weekends, she kept those plays going. People called her with all kinds of problems, and she solved them. When the director's babysitter didn't show up, my mother and I drove over; I warmed bottles, while she spooned applesauce into the baby's mouth. When the husband of one of the stars complained that his wife was away too much, my mother rushed to give counsel, later telling me word for word what happened. She seemed so incredibly alive. Watching her sing as she piled the shopping bags into the trunk, I smiled. She smiled back, reached over and pushed my hair up. "Just a simple pony tail would do it. You've got good cheekbones, good eyes — show them."

I was feeling stronger, and with my new clothes and new hairdo, other students began to notice me. I volunteered to do things, even as my heart raced in my chest. By the middle of sophomore year I was president of my home-room. I wrote for the school newspaper, and I made Boosters, which was like Cheerleaders except there were more of us, and we marched instead of cheered. In junior year I ran for secretary of the school. I campaigned hard, spoke in front of assemblies of a thousand students — and won.

Why was I doing all that? I believed it would help get me into college and medical school, but that was only a small part. I wanted to show my mother what I could do, prove my worth to her once and for all and be done with it. But the biggest reason was that having my name, my picture, in the school paper made me feel that I was good, important, better than normal.

On Saturdays I walked on Kings Highway with Harriet and Ann. That's when Bob came over; he knew Harriet's cousin. He was nineteen, with curly dark hair, clear skin and a cleft in his chin. He smelled of pipe tobacco, the tweed of his jacket, the oil from his car. He had a way of looking at me that got me excited and scared. Because of Rheumatic Fever, he just took a few classes at some college I didn't know. When he asked me out, I ran home and told my mother "I have a date for Saturday night. "

"Well, well, well — aren't you the sly one."

My mother darted in and out of my room, straightening the seams of my stockings, curling my ponytail, spraying me with her White Shoulders. When the door bell rang, she rushed to get it. She sat Bob on the green velvet sofa, got him a glass of soda, and sat in the wing chair beside him. "So, where are you in school?" She said, smiling.

"Adelphi, but I only take a few classes."

"A few classes? What are you going to do with *a few classes*?"

Bob's face turned red, and his forehead grew damp. I tried to catch his eye, but he was staring into his glass.

My mother lifted her head and looked out the window.

"Do you think the Dodgers will get the pennant again?" my father asked Bob, surprising me and my mother. "I like to hear what you young people think."

When I went to get my sweater, my mother stalked after me. "He's too old for you. He doesn't do anything. I don't like this."

He's nice. He's handsome. Nothing I do can please her. I'm tired of trying.

Bob and I went to a movie, and on the way home he stopped his car on the block before my house and kissed me, working his tongue into my mouth. I was surprised at how much I liked it, at what I wanted next. When he said he wanted to see me again on Wednesday I agreed, but told him we shouldn't meet at my house. I'd tell my parents I was doing something special for school. We went to his house, one of those big brick mansions on Courtelyou Road, and sat in a small downstairs room Bob called the parlor. He turned off the lights and pulled me onto his lap. When I told him I felt nervous, he rubbed my neck, my arms, my back with small, circular motions. He began kissing me. His hand went down the front of my dress, up under it. I buried my face in the warm, prickly skin of his neck. He wanted me to touch him outside his clothes, but I couldn't.

When he came over on Saturday my mother sat sewing in the wing chair. She looked like she was holding straight pins in her mouth. I had put on a sanitary napkin as protection against Bob. But after we started necking at his house, I went to the bathroom, rolled the napkin in toilet paper and dropped it in my purse. I saw him twice more and went through the same ritual with the napkin. When I got home after our last date my mother was waiting in the kitchen. She was wearing her blue robe, and her head looked oddly narrow with her hair in long metal curlers.

"If you get yourself pregnant," she hissed, "you can forget all your fancy plans. Forget College! Forget med school! Forget your life! If you get pregnant don't look to me for help. I won't lift one finger to help you." She reached backward for something, but her hands shook so wildly she knocked a pot cover to the floor. It rolled around on the linoleum, making a funny wobbling sound. We stood watching it.

I went to my room. *This woman is crazy. How can I get pregnant from what I'm doing?* I took off my sweater, and put it in the drawer that smelled of cedar. *Sperm were invisible. What if there were some on his hand! How long do they live anyway?* I hung my skirt on a metal hanger, almost doubled over from the ache in my stomach. I put on a long flannel nightgown that covered me from head to toe and stared at myself in the mirror. I liked how clean I looked with that white collar with tiny pink stripes high around my neck. I lay in bed rubbing my belly, thinking about Judy, a senior who'd gotten pregnant and dropped out of school. Everyone avoided her, giggled when they heard her name. And there were worse stories. Much worse.

I saw Bob once more, felt nervous and left early. When he called I told my mother to say I was out. She did it with gusto. He wrote, but his letters sat unopened in the cut glass bowl in the foyer. One day my father noticed that there were three letters from Bob.

"Why are these here?" he asked. "Why don't you answer them? This is no way to treat a person."

Scooping the letters from the bowl, my mother said, "This Bob is not a person."

While I was seeing Bob I was working at school on a clay head of an African woman I'd clipped from a magazine. I wanted to sculpt the way her nose, lips and chin made one perfect line. But when I unwrapped the head I saw that the nose was crooked. I wet the clay thoroughly and tried to straighten it. The face began to crack. I sat staring at the head. *My work is so sloppy. I let myself be distracted for nothing, for less than nothing.* It was late and the studio was empty except for me. In front where the tools were, I found an Exacto knife and returned to the statue. I sat on a high stool in front of the head and drew the blade across my thumb. A thin red line appeared. I felt excited, in charge of my life again. Later, I had a scar no one could see but me. It made me happy. I could touch it when I wanted.

Chapter 4. A Note from College

Early in my Freshman year, my first serious bout of anxiety brought me to Student Health. I'd been sent for personality tests, and a couple of days later the psychologist evaluating me asked me to deliver a bound manila folder to the psychiatrist who was to see me next. Feeling sure the file was about me, I biked to a soda fountain in Harvard Square, and ordered a chocolate egg cream. As I sat drinking it, I picked open the seal. This is what I saw.

PRIVILEGED AND CONFIDENTIAL

Dr. Carl Unger
Psychiatrist-in-Charge
Radcliffe Student Health
12 Garden Street
Cambridge, Ma 02138
Dear Dr. Unger: October 2, 1953

Thank you for letting me see your patient, Marjorie Tucker. My test results (enclosed) show that Marjorie has a well-organized personality. Her current anxiety, precipitated by her move to college, reflects her difficulty in forming a satisfactory adult identity. She fights identifying with her mother whom she views mainly as a shrew. Instead she attempts to identify with her idealized father. There is no evidence of suicidal thinking, or of any serious underlying problem. She's psychologically minded and should do well with brief therapy. If I can be of any further assistance please don't hesitate to call.

Yours sincerely,

Robert Pricewater Ph.D.

Chapter 5. Medical and other Training

In 1957, medical schools had a ten percent quota for women which most had trouble filling. Not that many women wanted to be doctors then, and many schools had off-putting ideas about women. At Harvard Med, my first choice, the brilliant female researcher who interviewed me asked if I planned to marry. When I said yes, she replied "We don't need dilettantes at Harvard." I ended up on their alternate list. At another school, a male doctor asked how I would function — on those, you know, odd days of the month. But my interviewer at Columbia College of Physicians and Surgeons assured me that they were happy with women students and knew how to treat them.

I left that interview knowing I'd gotten in, but despite these reassurances I was nervous. Female students were quickly ridiculed, and there was a story going around about a woman at Columbia who'd gotten upset in pathology lab and later found herself harassed by having cadaver testicles pinned to the back of her lab coat. My nervousness came back when my father helped move me into Bard Hall, the big dorm near the medical school. And it was still there on the Sunday evening before classes, as I sat in the dorm canteen, sipping hot chocolate.

A man with red hair asked to join me.

"Please do," I said, attracted by his cocky smile.

"Philip," he said, sitting across from me. He placed his Pepsi on the table and extended his hand. "And you're a freshman in medicine or nursing?"

"Marjorie. Medicine."

He pressed the cap back on his soda. "No kidding. First time I guessed wrong. You don't look like any medical student I've seen."

"And what exactly do you do?" I was angry about the speedy departure I saw coming.

"I'll be a junior in medical school — if I stay, that is."

"Is it that hard?" A nervous cough broke from me, making me spill my drink on the table. It missed Philip. Amused, he handed me napkins.

"It's not so hard," he said quickly. "If you got in, you'll make it through. If I leave it's because I'm — well — sort of disenchanted."

"Disenchanted? I can't even imagine that. Medicine's the only thing I've ever wanted. What's disappointing you?"

Philip sat thinking. He had a catlike face with neat, small features and blue-green eyes. "It's a long story," he said. "Not one for tonight. Besides, I'm more interested in a little problem I have right now. See, I kind of like you, but I could never let myself get really serious about a med student."

"Well, having discovered your mistake, please feel free to go." I busied myself cleaning the table.

"Is that what you want?" Philip leaned toward me. His eyes were tender.

"My concern is getting through med school. I'm not interested in plans that go beyond that." It was a lie, but I didn't want him to leave yet.

Balancing his chair on its back legs, Philip took a swig of Pepsi. We talked for a long time, and he made me laugh about the classes I'd be taking tomorrow. Later he walked me to my room and spent the night. I'd had a couple of affairs in college, brief unhappy ones with handsome campus Casanovas whom I didn't even like.

The next evening I brought my books to the lounge. I studied best when I could look up and see people. I read my assignments, then reread and underlined. I'd started reading what I'd underlined, when I spotted Philip at the front of the lounge. I stared into my book, so if he wanted, he could walk right past me. Soon I sensed him reading over my shoulder.

"Jesus, don't worry about flunking. You're going to ace the place." He pointed to a noisy corner where people were playing bridge. "That's where I'll be. Come by when you finish? We can grab a beer."

I nodded and watched the easy way he walked, his broad shoulders rounding forward with each step.

Later, when I reached the corner, he called out, "Wait just a minute while I bring this group to its knees." I waited a good twenty minutes. Then we went to a Pizza parlor across Broadway, and back to my room.

"Don't you ever study?" I asked him one night as I stepped out of my skirt.

"Since you've been around, I have studied some, but I made an even bigger change. I gave up my afternoon movies to attend lectures. See, your schoolmarm ways are rubbing off on me."

"You went to movies instead of lectures?" I stared at Philip who lay on my bed his head propped on one hand, the hair on his body glistening orange-red in the overhead light.

"I told you I was on academic probation. Now that doesn't just happen. You have to earn it."

I made a sour face. Philip laughed.

Making love was exciting, even though I never came. Philip had tried to bring me to a climax in different ways, but nothing worked. He seemed so disappointed I told him my contractions were so mild, I rarely felt them. I added that that was common in women, half believing it then myself. After making love, we went to sleep, our arms and legs folded together.

Our Biochemistry professor informed us one morning that radioactive carbon, an element I'd worked with that past summer, could cause leukemia. By the time I was back at the dorm, I felt tired, had aches in my arms and legs, and thought my lymph nodes were swelling. I kept checking them. Once I asked Philip to check them too. He carefully felt my neck, the groove over my collarbones, under my arms, and the long front crease where my legs joined my body. "You're fine," he said.

A couple of evenings later while we were studying in my room, my fingers kept kneading my throat. Philip slipped on his white jacket and said, "I'm going to take you to the Micro lab and test your blood. I'll prove there's nothing wrong."

"But, I can't do that."

"Why not?"

"Because if the needle you use has been improperly autoclaved, I could get hepatitis, which might be fatal, and all because I was trying to check on a leukemia I really don't have."

Philip shook his head like he'd just been swimming. "Congratulations. You've just raised medical student's disease to a new level."

I laughed at myself, grateful to have Philip to confide in. Whenever I worried that I'd flunked a test or made a fool of myself in class, Philip would sit me down, listen carefully, and diagnose 'Under Confidence Extremis.' "It's a bad case, Madame," he'd say. "You might consider treatment." Apart from times of anxiety, I liked school. I liked memorizing the names of bones, muscles, and the chemical reactions that ran the body. I even took pride in the faint formaldehyde smell that clung to my hands — proof I could dissect a cadaver.

When I told Philip that my leukemia scare had finally vanished, he took me out for beer and sausage pizza.

"Here's to a cured woman," he said, lifting his glass.

"Uh-uh, "I said "I know myself. I'll only drink to a remission."

Philip smiled briefly, then bummed a cigarette from a student at another table. He sat blowing smoke rings at the sooty tin ceiling. I knew by then that when he got into a non-talking mood, trying to get his attention only made him more remote.

I was watching people talking and laughing at other tables, when Philip touched my arm. "There are some things I need to tell you," he said. "My mom had two mastectomies. The second was right after I started Medical School. The first was three years before that, and her surgeon said that operation cured her. He says the same thing about this one, but now he won't answer specific questions." He shook his head. "It doesn't sound good."

I didn't know what to say and put my hand on his. He said his mother was cheerful, too cheerful. His dad was a wreck. And he was worried about his brother, Lawrence, who was only seven and didn't know anything was wrong. He talked on and on as though the words had been piling up for years.

"So this is what your disenchantment is about," I said.

"My disenchantment is self-pity — pure and simple. It disgusts me."

I squeezed his hand.

After that talk, Philip spent more time on the wards and in the library. Most often when I saw him in the evenings, he was bursting with the details of a difficult diagnosis he'd made, or how one of his suggestions had worked out. But if a patient went sour, or died unexpectedly, he'd berate himself or grow silent. He could sit through dinner barely saying a word. I knew he was thinking about his mother, but still his distance hurt. He'd apologize, and before the day was over, we'd be close again. Despite Philip's moodiness, and his swearing that he'd never marry a doctor, it was the first time I'd loved someone who loved me back. I felt more alive, happier than I could remember.

Sophomore year I worked with patients, learning to do physical exams and take medical histories. I was excited and worked hard to get everything right and remember every pearl the teachers dropped. It was Philip's senior year, and hospital after hospital rejected him for an internship because of his dismal early grades. He was miserable, and spent almost all his spare time playing bridge.

To keep from bugging him, I'd go home for an occasional weekend. My mother would follow me to my room, look me over, and say, "Still stuck on that boy who won't marry you? Five hundred men in that school and look who you pick. Why do you do these things to yourself?"

I'd take my books to the living room where my father sat in his club chair, reading.

When the internship assignments were announced, there was nothing for Philip. The Dean stepped in, made some calls and got Philip accepted at Jackson Memorial in Miami, a hospital with an excellent academic program. We celebrated by going to hear jazz that night in a club on Amsterdam Avenue. Coming home that evening, Philip invited me to join his family for his graduation dinner, and for a long weekend at his home in Providence.

I felt excited, but nervous about meeting Philip's family. Mrs. Roberts, Philip's mother, turned out to be a tall woman with sandy hair and a welcoming smile. She wore long sleeves, but when she worked in the kitchen I could see that her arms were red and tensely swollen. I wondered if they were as painful as they looked and tried not to stare. Philip spent the afternoons outside, playing ball with his brother. I'd sit by the flagstone fireplace then, reading. Whenever Mrs. Roberts spotted me by myself, she'd rush in ready to chat. I marveled at how she made everything feel complete, how good Philip must've felt growing up with her for a mother.

Philip left for his internship at the beginning of my junior year, when we began treating patients. I missed him all the time. It wasn't so bad during the day when I was busy, but in the evenings I felt lost and shaky. I called him almost every night. Sometimes I even thought of stopping medical school for a while so we could be together. Then slowly I befriended Bev, a transfer student from Philadelphia who'd moved in down the hall. Bev was a lively woman with curly brown hair, a chipped front tooth, and eyes that turned down at the corners making her look wise. And she was wise, or at least she had clarity and convictions. Science didn't come easily to her, but she was persistent, and unlike most other female students, not afraid to keep asking questions. We began having dinners together and long talks in the evenings. I felt steadier and my conversations with Philip grew less frequent, weekly or even less.

Bev was engaged to a Philosophy graduate student. I listened to all her plans with her fiancé, thinking — I'll never have that with Philip. Suddenly I was glad to have him at a distance. I wanted to meet other men. Most of my dates came to nothing, except for Ethan. He was a sunny-tempered man, one year ahead of me in medical school. Ethan was so much easier to be with than Philip that I literally prayed I could love him. But I couldn't even kiss him. I walked the tree-lined streets of Washington Heights wondering about myself.

Chap 6. Forced Choices

Philip invited me down to Miami on a bright spring weekend. As I walked through the gate, I saw him craning his neck, in an eager search for me. His hair had been cut too short, and patches of pink scalp showed wide around his ears. He'd lost weight and looked like the serious young men I'd see at airports with a baby perched against one shoulder. I felt a wild excitement.

We drove to his room near the hospital and immediately made love. During this brief, fumbling love making, I came. During dinner, I thought of telling him what happened, but didn't. I was glad I'd kept quiet because when we made love that evening, my old partially responsive self was back.

Philip asked me to come to rounds the next morning, saying his attending — the teacher on his ward — was eager to meet me. I smiled to myself, realizing he must've talked about me quite a bit.

Wearing a starched white coat that rubbed against my ankles, I followed Philip onto the ward at seven AM where we were joined by two yawning residents and the attending, Dr. Bigger, who had curly white sideburns and courtly Southern manners.

"Dee-lighted," he said, taking my hand in both of his. As we moved through the wards, I was astounded by Philip's knowledge. Usually residents are asked the questions the intern misses, but Philip did so well that Dr. Bigger had to think up new ones for them. I kept looking at Philip, thinking he'd changed. He'd grown up.

After rounds, Dr. Bigger ushered us to a lounge where a pot of coffee stood surrounded by thick white cups perched upside down on their saucers, like fat gulls taking the sun. He poured, and asked if I'd decided on a specialty yet.

"Immunology Research, I think." I was doing a research elective then.

"Splendid," he said. "Just splendid. Ah'd ask you more about it, but I know your answers would be ova mah head." Sitting back, sipping his coffee, he looked at me through half-closed lids. "So whaddya think of our boy heah desertin the work he's so good at to learn that Freudian malarky?"

My saucer clanked on the table. "You're going into psychiatry! That's wonderful."

Philip winked at the older man. "Told you she'd side with me."

"Why so secretive?" I asked Philip when we were back in his room.

"I'm a secretive kind of guy, you know that. And I've got even more secrets."

"Oh?"

"Guess where I'll be doing my residency?"

"Please — just answer." My heart was pulsing at my throat.

"N.Y.U. They had a last minute opening, and after seeing my recommendations from this place, they snapped me up. I got other acceptances too, but New York seemed well, more convenient." I started to kiss him, but Philip said I couldn't come to Miami without once seeing the ocean.

We drove quickly through palm-lined streets with small wooden houses, to a deserted spot on the beach. Standing out in the warm, green Florida Ocean, we made love. Philip had his cocky smile, but his eyes were tender. The water lapped around us, and I felt joyous and brazen and loved.

That night I woke up with a tightness in my chest. I looked behind the blinds at a soft black sky. The branch of some shrub was scratching back and forth across the window screen. I tried to ease my chest by breathing in-out, in-out, pacing myself to its slow rasping sound. Philip woke and asked what was wrong. I told him

I must be allergic to something. He gave me Sudafed which didn't help. We sat up holding hands then fell asleep and slept late into the morning. It was my last day in Miami. Philip pouted, then mocked himself.

We spoke frequently after that, planning all the things we'd do when he got back to the city. We each had our own triumphs to talk about. Philip had been named intern of the year, and I'd done so well on my medicine rotation that I was chosen, along with a handful of other students, to lecture to the second year class. I talked about the auto-immune disease, Lupoid Hepatitis.

To celebrate, my parents took me to Lundy's for a lobster dinner. We had one of our rare good times. "I like seeing you with a real smile," my mother said, looking at me with knowing eyes. "Is there something you're not telling us?"

"No, I just feel good."

Philip called as soon as he arrived in New York. "It's great here. I've got a roommate who'll be away another week. We've got a suite to ourselves. Come over, run over, fly."

I hailed a cab and sped down Fifth Avenue to Thirty-First Street. We met in the lobby of Philip's new dorm and raced to his room. As I pulled my sweater over my head, my chest grew tight. By the time I got it off, I couldn't breath. I told Philip something awful was happening inside me. He listened to my chest, took my pulse and blood pressure, looked into my eyes, and softly prodded my belly. "You're anxious," he said. "That's what all this is."

I sat in my beige slip, my back curved against the wall, feeling ashamed.

The next day I walked about on legs that could barely hold me. That had happened twice before — once when I entered college, and again when I left. The first time I'd rushed to Radcliffe Student Health and been told my symptoms would soon pass. They did; both times my anxiety started getting better after a week. But now, I kept on getting sicker. One weekend we had plans with another couple, and against Philip's protests we ended up seeing *Psycho*. I stayed only because if I screamed no one would notice. I'd developed frequent urges to run or scream. Philip found a psychiatrist for me. I was nervous, but went.

Dr. Samuels was a kind-faced man addicted to ties overrun by miniature horses. As I described my background, he listened intently and told me that I suffered from a lack of basic trust. I liked him and found myself eager to see him. With him, I could be totally honest.

One day, after we'd been talking about Yollie, he asked, "Well, how did it feel being dragged into that bathroom?"

"How do you think it felt?"

"I can imagine, but I want to know how it felt for you."

He wanted me to go back to that time, but I couldn't. I found just thinking about it humiliating. I don't remember a lot about our sessions, except that he wanted to talk about my feelings from the past, and I wanted to talk about my symptoms. When I cried about my fears of going crazy, he'd say, "You're really all right."

Then why do my legs feel like their collapsing under me? Why am I on the verge of screaming?

He suggested minor tranquilizers, which I refused. I was afraid medications would change me, dull my mind.

I spent most of my days on the wards or in my room. Harriet, my friend from high school, called and invited me to a lunch to meet her fiancé, Ira. He'd just been drafted and would be stationed in Europe for a year. I tried to get out of going, but she was insistent. That Saturday I took the BMT to Avenue M and walked to Harriet's house with its deep lawn and big picture window.

Harriet opened the door and kissed me, her face radiant. Harriet's mother, an abundantly cheerful woman, and my old friend Ann, kissed me too. Harriet introduced me to Ira, a slim man with dark hair and stand away ears. He was straightforward and likeable, much like Harriet. After filling my plate at the buffet, I sat in the half-circle of chairs watching Ira and Harriet greet new guests, while looking longingly at each other. I thought how easy their loving seemed and how comfortable I was sitting off to the side, talking with Ann. I stayed until they began moving the furniture back in place.

Walking back to the Avenue M station, I barely reached the corner before I felt dizzy. I stood there for a few minutes, then turned and walked to my own house.

"Are you staying for dinner?" My mother asked when she opened the door. When I said yes, she rushed up to Nostrand to get rib lamb chops. Some friends were coming over later to play bridge. As soon as the game started, I went in the den to watch TV. My mother looked in on me whenever she could. She knew I had problems, and had been eager for me to start treatment because a teacher friend of hers said being analyzed had saved her life.

"So, how's your treatment going?" Mom asked, perching on the daybed and lighting a cigarette.

"I'm not sure."

"Do you want to change doctors? If it's a question of money, I'll talk to your father."

"No, Dr. Samuels is fine. I just thought it would go faster."

My mother sat back, chewing her lip and smoking. "If it's money — speak up. You should never scrimp on either butchers or doctors."

I laughed at the way she said it. She smiled and went back to her game. Much of her sadness and anxiety had gone, and with it her harshness.

I slept late the next morning. After breakfast, I sat in the living room with my father, both of us reading parts of the *New York Times*. I knew I should go back to the dorm or call Philip, but thinking about him made me tense.

The sun was setting when I found Philip pacing in front of the lounge. I apologized, and we went to my room. As soon as I closed the door, my heart started racing. I knew it was ridiculous, but I was scared to be alone with him. I didn't know what else to do so I told him.

"It's okay," he said, working to calm himself down. "I understand. See if you can relax a little."

He sat on my bed, and I sat at the desk chair, staying as far from him as I could. If he moved suddenly, I jumped. Philip looked sad. I felt totally crazy.

Every time we got together my panics came back. He tried to help. But I began to think that his tenderness was feeding my terror — that he was making me sick.

Bev said, "Come to grips with it. If you run from Philip, you'll spend your life running from love." Dr. Samuels said I shouldn't do anything until I understood what was making me so anxious, but no matter how much he prompted me, I couldn't see beyond my symptoms. He again suggested meds. Again I refused.

When I arrived on the ward, the attendings took one look at me and asked what was wrong. They said I looked pale and suggested I stop by Student Health. I didn't go. What if they discovered how anxious I was? How crazy? After a couple of awful weeks of ducking attendings and pretending to be normal, I called Philip. I told him I needed a break from him — at least for a while.

"Let's play it by ear," he said. "This'll pass. Your panics always pass. And I'm here for you."

I kept on getting sicker. I had trouble just getting out my door. Usually I made it to work, but often skipped dinner. If I did that often, Bev dragged me to the cafeteria. I barely slept and cried frequently. My mind was on a young woman, a competent hospital secretary, who'd been brought to the psych ward while I was there on my clerkship. She'd never been sick before, but suddenly she was screaming obscenities and grabbing at the orderly's penis. *How long until I stepped over that line?*

It was 1960. The ward psychiatrists taught that anxiety like mine — high level and continuous — often signaled a breakdown to come. Dr. Samuels said I wouldn't lose control, but if I pressed him, asked how he could be so sure, he had no answer. In the psychiatric world there were few answers about extreme anxiety then. The division between psychosis and neurosis was crumbling as psychiatrists wrote papers describing highly anxious patients who looked neurotic, didn't improve with treatment, and did lose control. Every time I read one, I'd picture myself being rolled onto the ward, grabbing at the breasts or penises of people I'd worked with. I confessed this to Philip.

"I know you," he said. "It simply won't happen."

I desperately wanted to believe him, but when the panics hit, anything seemed possible. One night I called him and said, "I can't see you any more. I'm not sure this will help, but I've got to do something."

"But that's crazy, really crazy. Keep working with your doctor. These things take time."

"You don't know how sick I am," I kept repeating no matter what he said.

I didn't hear from Philip for almost a week. Then he took to calling me every night around midnight, asking if we could get together just to talk. I wanted to see him but felt afraid. At the beginning of December, his calls stopped completely. My anxiety drained from me followed by a sadness that made me feel dead. I dragged myself around for months, trying to accept a life without marriage or children — a life that wouldn't make me crazy.

Chapter 7. Michael

At the beginning of my senior year something inside me rebelled. Each morning I put on earrings that dangled with pearls and crystal, outlined my eyes with a thick dark pencil, and left the dorm swaying on spiky black heels that made my legs look good. The Columbia yearbook, class of 1961, shows me in my hunting clothes, eyes edged black as Cleopatra's.

My next assignment was Internal Medicine at Columbia's division at Bellevue. When I first got there, I saw a man in the hall with straight light brown hair, dark fringed hazel eyes, and a determined, in-command expression that made me wonder who he was. When I got to my ward, I discovered he was Michael, one of the residents there — the best resident there, the one the nurses turned to every time a patient coughed up blood or slumped over unconscious. He'd rush over, hold the patient with one arm, examine him with the other, while calling out for this or that medication. Against the odds, he brought many of those patients back. I watched him day after day, admiring his long square-edged fingers, the strong arms that could support a patient for hours. And there were some patients, tough men, who only trusted Michael. That impressed me too.

When I examined my first patient, an ex-sailor, Michael introduced us, saying "Watch your language. You're dealing with a lady now." Each night I'd rush back to the dorm to recount Michael's exploits to Bev. Later we'd go over his every word to me, looking

41

for some sign of special interest. "We may not get through this," Bev would joke. Then right before my rotation ended, I got a call at the dorm and a determined voice said, "How about coffee tomorrow?" It was Michael.

We met at a diner with white cloths on the tables.

"So, what do you like to do when you're not working?" Michael asked, a trace of perspiration gleaming on his upper lip.

"Read," I said. "I read a lot. Novels mostly. I'm always interested in the end of the story — you know, how people's lives work out."

"Interesting," Michael answered. "My brother reads a lot too. He's an English major."

The following year Michael was going up to Columbia for a Cardiology fellowship. He wanted to teach, do research, be a professor. As he spoke, I watched those long fingers point up, splay out, tap lightly at the table.

"And what about your plans?" he asked.

"Maybe medicine or psychiatry. I'm still not sure."

"Well, you'd be good." He wiped his mouth with a napkin. "Damn good."

We made a date for Friday night, and Michael picked me up at the dorm in a shining white convertible. Heading up to Bear Mountain, he drove fast and well. We went to a Japanese restaurant, where we cooked slivers of steak in a pot of sizzling oil. For each of our dates, he had a plan. Next we went to Stockton Inn in New Jersey right across the Delaware from New Hope. Michael said he'd just treated a man with a black eye, using a new enzyme that melted clots. "Did it work?" I asked.

"I'm not sure — the black and blue just spread across the man's face." He shrugged his shoulders and smiled. I laughed, but I was worried about my panics coming back.

After our third dinner out we went to Michael's apartment, a small studio with a closet-sized kitchen. His bed was carefully made with a tight navy blanket. Talking and drinking wine, we leaned against big red corduroy pillows. Michael kissed me. A quick light kiss. I kissed him back, and he turned the lights out. We were kissing and fumbling, and trying to undress each other. Then we both turned shy.

We undressed ourselves and got under the covers. Michael's body, what I could see of it, had long hard muscles. Sex was over fast. Michael said, "Oops. Give me twenty minutes. If I'm asleep, you wake me."

He curled toward the wall, and soon was snoring softly. I watched his back for a while and decided not to wake him. I'd had enough excitement for one evening. I looked up at the ceiling watching the flickering patterns cast by the neon signs on Second Avenue. I was only a few blocks from Philip's dorm, but I pushed that out of my mind.

In the morning Michael showered and shaved before I was up. He wore a crisp blue shirt, and with his straight shining hair and high-bridged nose, he reminded me of someone British. He'd bought grapefruit and orange juice, and small boxes of different cereals. He stuck one bag of freshly ground coffee under my nose, then another."

"Sniff. Which do you like better?"

I couldn't quite believe that this man I'd been dreaming about for weeks was really with me.

Making love again that morning was different — it went on for a long time, but didn't excite me. I didn't know if it was the rhythm or the timing, or my worries about getting anxious. Michael wasn't big on cuddling either. I was disappointed, but it made me worry less about my panics. Everything else was going the way I wanted, and I was grateful.

After we'd been dating for three weeks, we were walking on First Avenue. Michael drew in his breath and announced that he was serious, serious enough to talk marriage. I wanted to shout yes, but I had to be honest.

"I'm serious too," I said. "That's why I've got to tell you some things."

Michael put his hands in his pockets and looked ahead, his face tense.

"I think I may have some trouble loving. Once I …"

"What are you saying? You don't love me?"

"No, that's not it at all."

His face softened and his eyes looked up and to the side, the way they did when he was dealing with patients. "Then what is it — you can't be loyal?"

"No, but ..."

"You don't want a family?"

"That's not it."

He took my arm. "Oh, Marge, you just have some romantic ideas about love. That's all."

"Well, there's one other thing," I said. "I get anxious, sometimes so anxious I can barely function."

"Why are you saying these things?"

"Because I do get very anxious."

"Look, I'm a big boy. I don't expect perfection. We'll be fine."

Michael's certainty gave me courage. I still thought of him as sort of a god, and here was god promising me exactly what I wanted. We rushed to his apartment and called my parents, his, then our friends. On the ward the next day, people toasted me with wine in paper cups. The nurses told me about their weddings and showed me their rings. My heels clicked on the marble floors as I raced through the hospital corridors gathering up congratulations.

I hadn't spoken to Philip in six months. He must have heard the gossip, because he rushed up to Columbia and found me in an emptying classroom. I was startled to see him, looking so vivid with his broad shoulders and reddish hair. He kept asking why I played with him like that? He demanded an answer, but there was nothing I could say. I held my arms out to him. He slapped them down. He said he hated me, that he was glad things with us never went further. There was a blackboard behind me. I stood against it as Philip called me slut, whore, user. Then he was gone and I felt numb.

Two weeks later, I worked to put the scene with Philip behind me as Michael and I drove to have coffee with his parents, Bud and Cele. They lived in a woodsy section of Queens in a big one-family house with pine trees on the lawn. I was wearing my best dress, a black knit, but just before we left I discovered the lining hung down. I cut it with scissors and kept reminding myself to be sure that cut edge didn't show.

Cele hugged me at the door and blew a kiss past my ear. I breathed in powder and flowery perfume. A plump shapely woman, she led us into the living room where furniture upholstered in white satin was covered with thick clear plastic. Before us, on a round parquet coffee table, were platters of cut fruit and cookies stuffed with nuts, raisins, and chocolate. I sat nervously on the plastic, holding a cookie with one hand and tugging my dress over the lining with the other. Bud looked dapper with his thin moustache, a silk paisley scarf tucked into his shirt. He gave us a choice between sherry and schnapps.

"We've got more," Cele said. "We've got whatever you want." Michael and I took sherry. Bud had a scotch and soda, and Cele got ice water for herself.

"So," she said, sitting opposite us with a bright smile.

"So," Bud repeated, lifting his glass. "This calls for a toast to the happiest couple in New York."

Cele asked me questions. Where my mother taught —Lincoln High School; the name of my father's firm — Marshall, Bratter, Green, Allison, & Tucker; was my father the Tucker of "& Tucker" — Yes. With each of my answers Cele's eyes widened and she turned to Bud, who'd make a what-does-it-matter face.

"Bud owns a paint store," Cele said, lifting her chin. "Retail and wholesale. And me, well — since the boys have gone — I shop. Michael doesn't like me to say that. It embarrasses him."

When Michael went to the kitchen to get a Coke, Cele slipped into his seat and touched my arm with damp, cold fingers. "You're not — well, you're nicer than I expected. I hope we can be friends."

"Of course we can." At that moment all my worrying about the dress seemed silly.

After Michael came back, I paid careful attention to Cele, and when we left she planted a real kiss on my cheek. I kissed her back.

In the car Michael said his mother had this big thing about not going to college. It was silly. She was bright, and it was only a question of money. "She needs a lot of reassurance," he said.

The next evening, coffee was at my parent's house. My mother opened the door and spread her arms wide. She was wearing an emerald silk dress that showed off the creamy whiteness of her skin. Her earrings were golden stars, each with a central pearl. She hugged me, but somehow Michael stepped to the side, and they ended up shaking hands. As she led us to a coffee table laden with food, I walked behind Michael, thinking this man is intelligent, nice, handsome, going places and HE WANTS ME. I sipped my wine as my mother asked her questions. I watched her smile and nod as Michael rattled off Yale, Harvard Med, The Columbia Division of Bellevue. Her face was fuller then, her hair colored a soft blond. She asked Michael about his family, but when his answers were brief, her smile disappeared. She glanced at me, took a deep breath, and in an animated voice told Michael stories about our family — who came from Russia and when. How my father clung to his mother on the boat all the way from Russia. "I was only two," my father said, laughing. Michael smiled slightly at times, but made few comments. When we left my mother held out her hand. My stomach ached.

I had Michael drive me back to my dorm, so I could call her in private.

"You don't like him," I said.

"Cold. Margie, he's too cold for you."

I asked my father what he thought, and he said, "I barely know the man."

I told Bev that I was angry at my parent's response. I said Michael was shy, not cold. Bev said they were probably upset because I was moving so fast. "Three weeks isn't enough time to get engaged. Do you really know Michael?"

I sat in my dorm room, looking at my bookcase. I did know Michael. I knew what was important — he'd stand by me, he didn't see me as damaged, and he helped me feel calm. I'd done a lot of thinking about why I'd panicked with one man, and not so long after, was comfortably marrying another. The most obvious answer was that Philip wanted a wife who'd stay at home. But when I let myself be honest, I knew I was less frightened by Philip's needs than mine. Sometimes with Philip I pictured putting medicine aside and being happy. And there were other dangers too, ones that it took me years to put into words. Philip could mean everything to me. He could be my world, so if he left me, or stopped loving me, I'd be nowhere. But Michael held me at arm's length, so with him, I had to stand on my own two feet. And he wanted me to be a doctor; our marriage would work best if I was one.

Around Easter my mother invited Michael and his family to dinner. I had a ring by then, a fire opal, and my wedding was set for just before my graduation, a small ceremony in a judge's chambers.

My aunt Beaty arrived first. She pulled herself up the front stairs with one crutch, while I held the other one. After sitting down, she took my hand and asked if I was happy. "Yes," I said. "Very." Michael's brother, Todd, came next. He was a sophomore at Williams College, a short, wiry man, who looked nothing like Michael. He handed my mother three red roses. Then came my aunt Mollie, the sister born between Beaty and my dad, with her husband Mike. They were both teachers with movie star looks. Beaty called them, "The hot couple."

While I was helping my father fill drink orders, Michael phoned. He said to make some excuse — he'd be late. Cele was still running up and down the stairs changing outfits. I told my mother that Michael's car had stalled. No problem, she said, the brisket was still in the oven. She took her apron off, wiped her face, and sat down with the guests.

About a half-hour later the doorbell rang. This time Michael stood stiffly, allowing my mother to kiss him. Cele stood behind him, a mink stole around her shoulders, her short brown hair combed up like a tiara. Bud was beside her, a big cake box in his hands.

When we sat down to eat, Beaty, a bacteriologist at Bellevue then, swapped hospital stories with Michael. Todd had come from seeing *The Seventh Seal* for the third time and talked about Bergman's symbols. Whenever there was a lull in the conversation, Bud told stories that ended with "Was you there, Cholly?" Even my father told some jokes. My mother sat with her elbows on the table, her face flushed, her lips open in an enormous smile. When she caught my eye, she winked and waved her hand as if to say — Look how they're coming together. I winked back.

After coffee, Cele called Michael into the living room and spoke to him in a low voice. She looked worried. Michael answered quickly, then left her standing by herself. I went over to her, but as we talked her eyes followed Michael. She looked young with the makeup gone from her face. Later, back at Michael's apartment, I asked him what happened.

"Nothing," he said. "Just her usual need for constant reassurance."

"So why didn't you give her some?"

Michael didn't answer. He sighed and opened one of his books.

That night Michael began telling me stories about Bud and Cele. He turned off his reading lamp and spoke in a low voice. He said his father used to be away for days. He was less than five then; Todd wasn't born yet. Cele would dress Michael up, make his favorite foods, and in the evenings they'd listen to the radio nestled together. Suddenly Bud would sweep into the house, rush upstairs and call for Cele. She'd put a big piece of chocolate cake on the kitchen table, and disappear for hours. When she did check on Michael, and that might be late at night, she reeked of sweet perfume. He said it was years before he figured out what was happening.

After telling these stories, Michael rose wordlessly from his chair, flossed his teeth in the bathroom, went to bed, and quickly fell asleep. It seemed that I now knew why Michael was so annoyed with Cele, and I wanted to help him deal with it. That was a time when I thought knowing your problem brought you close to solving it.

For several days I wondered how to bring it up, until Michael gave me an opening. I'd made buttermilk pancakes, and while eating a big syrup-soaked stack of them, he said, "You know, Cele's no kid, but she still looks good." He sighed, then shook his head as if puzzled by something.

"Maybe you're still angry with her for all the things that happened?"

"What things? What are you talking about?" Michael held his fork in the air.

"Those stories you …"

"I told you personal stories, in private. I never expected you to repeat them or weave them into some sick theory of yours." Michael looked at me with burning eyes, daring me to add a word.

I ate my pancakes.

After we cleaned up in silence, Michael went out shopping for food. I sat on the sofa feeling sick. Mostly I felt guilty about wounding him — betraying his trust. But it was like me to delve into people's insides. "Creeping inside someone's *kishkes*," my mother called it. I'd always done it, and it would happen again. Was our life together going to be a disaster? I called Bev. She'd come to like Michael, and I wanted her to tell me how wonderful he was. I couldn't bring myself to tell her exactly what happened, so I rambled on as she listened.

After hanging up, I sat thumbing through a magazine. I felt numb and empty and my chest was tight. Michael burst through the door, his cheeks red from the cold. He was smiling and held his hand out. "Come on, let's go shopping. We'll need lots of things for our apartment. It'll be fun."

We went to Macy's and soon got caught up comparing patterns of dishes and glassware. We picked up forks and knives to feel the heft of them in our hands. Later we went to dinner with friends and Michael was charming. By the end of the evening, I knew I belonged with him. Driving home, I gazed into my opal.

Chapter 8. Problem Patients

By the end of medical school I knew psychiatry was my calling. My residency at Columbia Psychiatric Institute went well, and at the end of my first year I wanted to apply for analytic training.

Being a psychiatrist and an analyst are two distinct professions, although back in 1962 they were not as different as they are today. Back then, to be accepted at an Analytic Institute, you had to be psychiatrist, or have started to become a one. At an Analytic Institute you completed a special analysis — a training analysis — and analyzed three patients under supervision. The training analysis was conducted by a senior analyst who periodically reviewed your progress with a promotions committee, making many psychiatrists reluctant to pour out their troubles.

I wanted to go to the Columbia Psychoanalytic, the Institute associated with my residency. I had good recommendations, got good grades in my classes, but Dr. Samuels, the analyst I'd been seeing when I had those panics over Philip, felt entering the Institute would be a mistake for me. He said I'd had so much trouble looking at myself, that before applying, I should have a couple of years of personal analysis and try only after that went well. I thought his comments over, but was ambitious and eager to keep up with my classmates. And part of me believed I was fine — just fine. I met with Dr. Samuels a couple of times and convinced him I'd made major changes.

I'd been happily married for two years. I'd finished medical school with a good record. I had anxiety, but no panics. But sometimes I wondered if I'd really changed that much. I didn't know why my panics came and went. I didn't really understand why I'd panicked over Philip. And at some level I knew I needed help. Yet I ignored my doubts, applied and was accepted. But I wasn't fine and that became painfully clear to me when, as a second year resident, I treated a patient who affected me in ways I never expected.

On a hot July day in 1962, I walked up to the Acutely Disturbed ward to meet Wendell, one of my new patients. His former resident couldn't wait to be rid of him and warned me to keep my distance. Wendell, a college freshman, had been admitted six months before after cutting both his wrists. He settled into the unit quickly and appeared well, but every time there was talk of moving him to a less protective ward, he'd find a pillow case or towel and try to hang himself. Although the staff felt these were manipulative gestures, they were still afraid to move him. Their other choice was to send him to the big state hospital at Rockland, but they didn't do that either. So there he sat, this seemingly well man on our most heavily-staffed unit.

I was sitting in the nurse's station reading through Wendell's chart when the chief resident came over, cleared his throat and said, "If you can't move him downstairs in a few months, he's going to Rockland."

"Does he know that?"

"We figured you could tell him."

I swallowed my anger as an aide led me to a tiny room. Behind him was a young man with clear white skin, curly brown hair, and innocent chestnut eyes. His beautiful face was oddly mounted on a boxer's thickened body. "So how long will you be my doctor?" Wendell asked politely.

"I'm here for another two years."

"Then private practice I bet. Upper West Side? Well, am I warm?"

Suddenly he smiled. Wendell was distractingly appealing, and to make matters worse, we sat facing each other in a room so small that our knees were almost touching. Adopting my most professional manner, I said, "We should talk about your future."

"But yours is funner, Doc. Me, I'm just staying here."

I hesitated, then told Wendell about his new choices. He sat in silence, tapping his foot on the floor. After a while, he asked to be excused and came back smoking. His hand, big with swollen knuckles, shook as he moved the cigarette back and forth from his mouth.

"You know, I'm good here," he protested. "I help with the sicker patients, and I know if I ever get really angry, three guys will come at me with a mattress. This is where I belong."

"It wasn't my decision."

Wendell sat shaking his head and sighing.

I watched him for a while. Then said, "Why not try to get better?"

Wendell looked at me, his surprise edged with contempt. "Doctor, did you read my chart? Did you read about how I almost killed my father, the stuff about my sister?"

"I read your chart from cover to cover."

"And you think I can make it outside?" Deep lines appeared on his forehead.

"You were making it outside until you got here."

He shook his head. "Not really. I cut my wrists more than once, and I was getting incompletes."

I felt confused — sweat formed at the back of my neck. "That wasn't in your chart."

"When I first got here I wasn't sure what I wanted, so I didn't spill out everything."

"And now you know what you want?" *A locked ward for life.*

Wendell's face grew paler. "No. It's more that now I see my future. I nose out what really bothers people, then the next thing I know, I use it against them. I hurt my sister, my girlfriend, my room-mates, my first resident. If you try to help me, I'll hurt you too."

I heard Wendell's words, ones recited so flatly he could've been reading from a manual, but behind them I sensed him pleading with me to take him on and stick with him no matter what. I liked him, but more than that — I had to save him.

Psychiatric Institute was part of the large complex of buildings that made up Columbia Presbyterian Hospital and Medical School in Washington Heights. The Institute was a large brick building with marble floors that always seemed clean. It was built on a hill that ran down to the Hudson so the front entrance opened onto the tenth floor. The administrative offices were on ten or above, but most of the hospital, including the wards, was below. The acutely disturbed ward came first, housing the fewest patients. Ward six, the one I wanted for Wendell, was under that, a locked unit with less supervision and outside passes as patients improved. Further down were the open wards where patients came and went.

As summer cooled to fall and leaves dropped from the trees, Wendell arrived on ward six. Most patients there were heavily medicated Schizophrenics and Manic-Depressives. Wendell took the place over. With amazing accuracy he identified simmering staff feuds and brought them to a boil. Staff members suddenly stopped talking to each other, and we needed extra meetings just to keep the ward going.

I didn't have a clue about what Wendell was doing, or even a name for what he had. Today we'd say Wendell had a Borderline Personality Disorder and was *splitting* the ward into warring factions — unconsciously leading staff members to take opposing sides in his inner conflicts.

Dr. Marcuso, the assistant ward chief, a young balding man who worked best with Schizophrenics, was assigned to supervise me. "Get rid of him," he said at our first meeting. "He's causing too much trouble. No hospital can help him"

I argued with Marcuso, saying Wendell could be helped and besides he was chronically suicidal. He disagreed. He said if Wendell really wanted to do it, he would have.

The first thing I did after that supervision was talk with Seaman. He was a one-eyed black aide on ward six who knew more about patients than almost anyone around. He agreed that Wendell should be there. He told me that Wendell had taken a liking to Charles, a retarded boy. He protected him from teasing and worked to cheer him up. Also when Wendell thought no one was watching, he scraped his arm with a razor or banged his fist against the bathroom wall.

On the subway, going to my own session, my mind was on Wendell. My training analysis with Dr. Easser had just started and she'd quickly become my idol. She was married with four children and astounding at her work. About six feet tall, with a long attentive face and straight dark hair that curled under at the ends, she looked awkward yet lovely. I believed she knew me better than I knew myself. I saw her four times a week and told her stories, reported daily events, but when she waited for something more my mind went blank.

But that day was different. I sat down and asked for her help with Wendell.

"I'm not here to supervise you," she said, tapping her pen against her chin. "But, I am interested in why you're so drawn to this boy, and how Michael feels when you get so involved with a patient?"

"You don't understand," I practically yelled at her. "All this boy can see is his own rage, but I know he can love. I've got to make him see himself the way I do. Please, help me just this once."

Dr. Easser continued tapping her pen. I knew she was waiting for my answer to *her* question.

A few weeks later, I went to a staff meeting on ward six where the subject was Wendell. He was still hurting himself and causing more staff problems. Marcuso wanted him in Rockland, but I argued that his only chance was to continue with us. Half the staff agreed with me; half sided with Marcuso. But the ward chief wanted to keep him. After the meeting, Marcuso took me aside and said, "Your stubbornness is going to get somebody hurt." That didn't bother me as much as what came next.

When Wendell came down to my office for his session, he looked angry. "You're going out on a limb for me. Why can't you protect yourself more?" I waited for him to go on, but he sat in silence looking at my rug. I asked him to talk about his anger at me, but he didn't answer. I sat in silence too. After a while, he lifted his head and scratched noisily at the stubble on his chin. The sound was pleasing. I found myself admiring his round white neck. He caught me looking, smiled for an instant.

That Friday we had our weekly community meeting on ward six. Most of the patients, the staff on duty, and residents with patients on the unit, came. We sat on folding chairs in a big circle. The head nurse started the meeting and the patients argued about who controlled the TV, and asked for afternoon naps. Then Wendell started talking. He talked about me. "Just look at her French twist. Must take her an hour to fix it. And those spotless silk clothes. See, no one can touch her, but she must get off on something. Maybe she takes those papers she's always reading home, rolls them up and..." He jiggled his fist by his groin. Everyone looked at me. I felt embarrassed and furious at Wendell.

He knew he'd rattled me and began hurting himself more. I asked Dr. Kolb, the head of the Institute, if we could talk about Wendell. He agreed; he was good that way. I told him what was happening on ward six and described Wendell's childhood. His mother was always out, he had fist-fights with his father, and his main comfort came from having sex with his retarded older sister. She was in an institution now, and Wendell blamed himself for that as well as for her being retarded. I also told Kolb about Wendell's problems with women, how when his last affair ended, he'd thrust a razor deep into his wrists.

This small older man who had written our textbook, drummed his fingers on his chair. "I have no magic answer," he said. "Try to work with him, but remember not everyone gets better. One of my patients hung himself last week."

I went home and talked about Wendell at dinner, although there was little Michael could say. Afterwards, I kept thinking about him while Michael read his journals. I was still thinking about him that Saturday as I stood outside Saks, waiting for Bev, my friend from medical school. She was pregnant and wanted company buying maternity clothes. On the escalator she kept asking what was wrong — were Michael and I having trouble? At the maternity section I made myself focus on how the dresses she was trying on complemented her skin tone, and how they'd look when she showed more. We walked to a luncheonette on Fifty-Seventh Street. Over grilled cheese sandwiches, Bev told me about making dinner for her in-laws. She'd gotten so nervous she served rubber hard shrimp over burnt rice. I was laughing, and for the first time in weeks, forgot about work.

Walking home through Central Park, it hit me. Wendell needed a goal — a reason for living. I told him that at our next session. He laughed and asked if that's how I kept myself going.

"In part," I said.

After the New Year, Wendell started wheeling a cart of library books from ward to ward. He listened carefully to what interested each patient, and asked how things went. He dressed up for this. His color was better, less like white marble, and he was hurting himself less. In the evenings he read to Charles.

Sometimes in session, Wendell sat looking at his hands, talking about the family he didn't see any more. He talked about fighting with his father when he was about sixteen and wanting to kill him. When he realized he could actually do it, he ran from him and using his bare fists, punched out every window of their house. He began telling me of other times when he'd turned his rage away from people. For the first time he seemed curious about himself, even optimistic.

That weekend, a long one, Michael and I went to New Hope for what we'd talked about as a romantic little vacation. We stayed in a bed and breakfast where our room had a goose down comforter and smelled from the wood fire below. But we didn't make love either night; we didn't even snuggle. I was thinking about that when Wendell came for his next session. He immediately asked what was wrong.

"Nothing. I'm tired."

He stretched his legs before him. "I know I tease you and all that. But you're okay, Doc. You're better than okay."

I felt so grateful, it shamed me.

It also shamed me that the highpoints of my week were my times with Wendell — that's when I felt most alive. I told this to Dr. Easser and her lack of alarm reassured me. She said I was blocking my deeper feelings, especially ones toward Michael. I heard her words, but had no idea what she wanted. It was like asking a blind woman what she sees.

By spring Wendell was well enough to go outside on passes. He signed up for a summer course at Hunter College in Abnormal Psych. He bought himself a light blue shirt and a sunlamp. I felt excited until he rolled his sleeve up and showed me what looked like a game of tic-tac-toe sliced into his arm.

"Jesus, why didn't you ask for me?"

"People can surprise you. This I can count on."

As he rolled his sleeve down, he must've seen disappointment in my face, because he stopped and said, "You're not going to keep me out of school for this? Because I wasn't trying to ... You understand?"

I nodded. I understood more than I wanted. I understood that after almost a year he still wouldn't let anyone in. I also knew that about once a year a seemingly well patient, much like Wendell, jumped from the George Washington Bridge into the Hudson River which was right behind us. I rushed to the coffee shop hoping to find somebody to talk with so I could forget what I was thinking.

Wendell was writing "A" papers, but he was more interested in Sandy, a busty young woman who smiled and saved him a seat. He talked about her constantly. I felt scared for him. When he started going to Sandy's apartment after classes, I grew even more frightened.

On Tuesday, the fourth week of class, he came back early and announced he was finished with school. He'd fought with Sandy. It grew heated and he compared her breasts to douche bags. She'd dropped the class. His face was rigid as he told me this.

I had an awful sinking feeling. We sat silently for awhile, then seeing the resignation in his face, I said, "Okay, we have to work on your problems with women. We'll start right away."

"How are you going to help me? I'm not some cold fish like you. I need someone to love me. I need to be touched. Say, how often do you and Hubby..."

"Just stop it."

Wendell fell back in his chair, crumpled up before my eyes.

"I can't make it outside," he said. "I really can't."

"Yes you can! This is just a temporary setback." *Slap him, shake him, hold him, kiss him. Do anything to pull him out of this.*

After Wendell left, I looked out the window and saw gray sky resting on the silky back of the river. The Hudson was wide there, its surface barely moving.

The next day Wendell told Charles he was dumb. Charles dropped to the floor and banged his head against it. While staff worked with Charles, Wendell ran into the bathroom and slammed his fist into the wall, shattering bone. I came up on the ward and waited while Wendell's hand was being set. I felt a pain in my stomach, and it got sharper when he came back and I saw the vacant look in his eyes.

I walked slowly back to my office. I sat at my desk feeling sick, but when I started to write my note, something inside me shifted. I saw that Marcuso was right: Wendell was not suicidal. He was manipulating me because I was over-involved with him. He was playing a game, but if I didn't play my hand, he couldn't play his. If I became impersonal, set firm limits, he'd get better. I knew this with a dreamlike certainty.

When I went to the ward, the head nurse said, "He's spinning out of control. It's clear what's coming next. He ought to go back upstairs for a while." I agreed. There were no beds until the next day, so I put him on observation.

The next morning, in a room on the ward, I told Wendell he was going back up to the acute ward. "Just for a while," I said in my new crisp voice.

"Leave me here, Doc. Bend the rules. You've done that before."

"It didn't help. No more bending rules now." I thought of myself as a surgeon. *Surgeons are relentless, they cause pain, but in the end they save the patient.*

"If you don't want me anymore, give me to another resident. No hard feelings, I understand."

"I'm just changing my treatment approach."

"Changing your treatment approach? You can't even look at me. LOOK AT ME. LOOK INTO MY EYES."

I looked into clear chestnut eyes with fine black lines streaming back from the pupils. When I started to see pain, I looked down at the dull white of his cast, but still I saw the pain. *Think surgeon.*

An hour later, the nurse called to say Wendell wanted an emergency session. I opened my office door and saw Wendell coming down the hall followed by an aide. He must've given himself a sunlamp treatment, because his skin was roasted pink above his tan. He stopped in front of me; our eyes met for one bizarre out-of-time second. Then, he ran out the emergency exit, and a siren went off. The aide raced out the door. I followed and stood holding it open while the siren wailed. When the aide came back alone, I called the police.

I sat at my desk, head high, pushing pins deep in my French twist, readying myself. Eventually the phone rang as expected.

"I'm right by the George Washington Bridge. Tell me you'll keep me on the ward and I'll come back."

"Come back."

He hung up, called right back. "Tell me I can stay on the ward or I'll jump right now."

"Come back." *Surgeons don't let themselves get distracted.*

Third call. "Just say *you'll* fight to keep me on the ward. Say that and I'll come back."

"Come back."

At rounds the next morning the staff was surprised Wendell was still out. We talked about the phone calls. Some of the residents said I should have agreed to his demands, especially the last one. Others said I was honest, and that'd be best in the long run. Each day at rounds there was a quieter tone, but everyone was still sure he'd be back soon. I didn't feel like a psych resident anymore; I didn't feel like a doctor. I spent my evenings and most of the next weekend at the hospital waiting for Wendell. At night, Michael would come to take me home.

Later that week, Wendell's body washed up on the shore. I was stunned, and not stunned. I took a day off to think about him. Then I went around telling his story to any supervisor who'd listen. They said I couldn't face his dying and offered bits of advice, but mostly they said it would've happened sooner or later. No one criticized me for how I handled his last calls, and that upset me. At night, I lay awake replaying those calls in my head. I'd picture him desperate and alone on the bridge and ask myself how I could have been so cold, so blind, at the end.

"Don't you see what you're doing?" Easser demanded, sounding angry. "You're running around trying to get yourself thrown out of the residency. Sure you made mistakes, but you've got to live with them. That's what it means to be a doctor."

Her words helped. I waited for her to say more. She leaned forward, her long face somber. "Look, there's something we should talk about. If your main goal is being an analyst, go back to the Institute. They'll reassign you. But if you want to work on yourself with me, quit your analytic training. You use it to hide your own problems." She sat back. "Take your time and think it over."

That night, a Friday, I talked things out with Michael. He said that since I wanted to be an analyst I should ask to be reassigned. Why let one doctor change my life? I agreed, and knew it would be embarrassing to quit the Institute. I couldn't sleep that night.

The next day I went for a long walk in Central Park over hot rocky trails near marsh ponds. If the new analyst was good I might end up in this same spot, except that doctor might not offer to keep working with me. And if the new doctor wasn't good, maybe I'd slip through, become an analyst with nothing fixed inside. Maybe I'd always turn off on patients. That idea was frightening, and I sat down on a rock to think about it. Maybe I'd learn not to turn off, but what would I be like? I wouldn't be like Easser with that poised way she had of taking so much in, then coming out with helpful, truthful answers. I tried to picture her, her marriage and her sex life. I'd seen her dancing at an Institute party. She had a sense of joy. Maybe I could learn that? I trusted her and knew she was pulling for me. When would I find that again?

I quit the Institute and spent my last residency year working with Dr. Easser as a private patient. Following that we were moving to Bethesda for Michael's research fellowship. It was a good year, allowing me to feel confident and gain a better understanding of some of the things that had happened. I'd seen myself in Wendell, but had trouble seeing how different we were. I didn't understand the depth of his pain or his aloneness. I needed him too much. I needed to feel he could be saved, and that I could save him. I turned away when it became clear I couldn't.

And I understood my marriage better. I knew I didn't get some important things I needed, but hoped that would change. I sensed Michael struggling to be warmer, less guarded. I'd help him bring that out. I knew we'd be all right if I was careful with my marriage, worked at it, protected it. Besides, I left New York nine months pregnant.

Chapter 9. San Francisco

My concerns about moving to Bethesda were overshadowed by my worries about having a baby. I was afraid I wouldn't be able to nurse, or even sufficiently love my own infant, but all that stopped as soon as I saw him. Being near Keith, holding him, watching him roll and sit brought out feelings I'd never expected. Michael was busy with his research, but excited to have this eager-eyed son who he'd carry high in one hand, saying, "That's a car, that's a dog, over there's a Chinese restaurant."

In Bethesda, I was surrounded by people. First my parents, then Michael's, rushed down to greet their new grandson. Friendly young families, transients like us, filled our building, and if I wanted company at any time, I could go to the lobby or laundry room. When Keith was six months old, I wanted to return to part-time work but was reluctant to leave a baby with a sitter. After Sandy, a woman I knew from the building agreed to watch him, I began working in a small mental health clinic on Hampden Lane, doing treatment and evaluations. One of the social workers there, Liz Hirsch, was the wife of Seymour Hirsch, Eugene McCarthy's first campaign manager. Through her, I got involved in the Vietnam War protests and campaigning for McCarthy. I'd take Keith and drive to Washington where I'd push him in his stroller, walking beside staff from my clinic with their small children. I felt so important then: I was at the center of my child's life and close to the center of a movement I thought would change the world.

When we began our third and last year at Bethesda, I thought we'd look for work in New York. But before we even started, one of Michael's former teachers offered him a tenured position at the University of California Medical Center at San Francisco, adding that they'd find something for me too. This was a hard offer to turn down, but then Michael announced that San Francisco was exactly where he wanted to be. New York, he claimed, was dirty and dangerous. I protested that we'd be leaving our families and friends, but Michael said, "Look, a good five year try is all I ask. If you want to go after that, we will. But you won't want to. It's like paradise there."

Reluctantly, I gave in.

I tried to take pleasure in that gorgeous city of bay views, pastel houses, and gardens lush with purple fuchsia and cobalt blue lobelia. I'd take Keith to the Palace of Fine Arts in the Marina, to the Zoo, and on the ferry to Sausalito. But near home, an apartment in Pacific Heights, I could walk around an entire block and see maybe one other person. I felt lonely and cold, and it was an odd coldness that wasn't helped by a warm day or sunny sky. Keith asked to be with other children so I enrolled him in a pre-school program.

But meeting new people at my age wasn't easy. Michael was settling into a department filled with competitive new doctors, and I didn't have an actual job for a while. Leo Rothstein, Vice Chairman of Psychiatry at Langley Porter, the Psychiatric Hospital at U.C., suggested I take a position that amounted to being a glorified secretary, explaining that in his experience women didn't like taking orders from other women. When I refused, he had me going from office to office trying to sell my services to people who had no positions. Finally one of the senior professors, Jurgen Ruesch, made a place for me as a research fellow. It was a good position, but since I spent most of my time sitting in my office reading, it didn't decrease my isolation. But I did get friendly with Richard, the orthodox Jewish psychiatrist who was Ruesch's other fellow.

I hardly expected an orthodox Jew with a beard and yarmulke to be open minded and funny, but Richard was. Tall, with round, pink cheeks, and teasing brown eyes, he had a smile that always made me want to smile back. We were both busy developing our research plans but talked whenever we could. Often we had lunch together, Richard eating something his wife had fixed for him.

One cool August afternoon when I entered the library in the main medical building, my heart started racing, my legs shook, and I felt sure I'd pass out. I made it back to my office and called Michael. He came right over and checked me. "You're fine," he said. "Probably some minor transient problem." And I did feel better when he called later. I didn't think of anxiety because I hadn't had a panic since leaving Dr. Easser, three years before. But, a few days later when another attack came, I knew my panics were back. I couldn't understand it. I believed then that one good analysis resulted in a cure.

Michael had seen me nervous, preoccupied, obsessing, but never in an outright panic. He couldn't believe it was psychological; at his insistence I had a complete medical work-up, but nothing was found. When Michael saw me in a panic — and that was rare because I tended not to panic when he was around — I could see his confusion, his helplessness, and the embarrassment he worked to hide. I was ashamed of my condition too. No one talked of fighting the stigma of mental illness then. We just worked to hide our symptoms, especially if we were doctors, and most especially if we were psychiatrists.

While walking in the hall at Langley Porter one afternoon, I started to tremble and felt a scream pressing at my lips. I rushed to Richard's office, knocked on his door, and as soon as I saw him, felt relief. He sat me down and listened patiently as I went on about my panics and my treatments. "Get back in treatment," he said finally. "After all, San Francisco is therapist central."

When I started to leave his office, I felt anxious again. I told him I was afraid I'd lose control and scream in the hall.

"Don't worry. I'll leave my door open, and if you scream, I'll run out screaming behind you. Everyone will follow us. It'll be fun."

Later, if I did feel tense while walking in the hall, I'd calm myself by picturing the staff running out behind us, shouting and waving their arms like gospel singers.

A week later I went to see a well-thought-of San Francisco analyst, Dr. Alfred, who had an office in one of the big Victorian houses on Sacramento Street. A pug-nosed man with short curly hair, he puffed his pipe as once again I poured out my story. Certainly he could help. All I had to do was come three times a week, lie on his couch, and say what came to mind.

Dr. Easser never put me on her couch, and when I asked why, she said it would make me more anxious. I told that to Dr. Alfred, but he said, "It's the only way I work. It makes for a better analysis."

Disappointed my work with Dr. Easser hadn't helped me more, I saw the appeal of the more traditional method. But lying on the couch with only the ceiling to look at made me dizzy. I'd prop myself on my elbow and turn to where Dr. Alfred sat behind me, puffing his pipe. He'd take it from his mouth and use the still wet stem to gesture me back down. "Tell me what's coming to your mind," he'd say. What was coming to my mind was wanting to shake him until his eyeballs rattled, because while I was getting sicker all he was doing was saying "Hello" and "Time's up." I'd tell him that, and he'd answer with another puff on his pipe.

Michael would go to sleep around ten, and I'd sit in the living room with the TV on, thinking about my treatment. Usually I felt better at the end of my sessions with Dr. Easser, but Dr. Alfred's silence was making me anxious and angry. And the more I thought about it, the angrier I got. Sometimes I'd get so worked up, I'd call him at home, but when someone answered, I hung up.

I went to session one day and said, "You know all those hang ups you get at night? Well they're from me. Please do something more because I hate myself for calling like this — I'm getting sicker. I know it."

Puff. Puff.

After my confession, I managed not to call him anymore and tried to convince myself that getting sicker was only a stage in getting better. My greatest fear then was that I was too sick to be analyzed and would have these panics forever. I'd lie on the couch, one foot on the floor to help with my dizziness, and talk about how bad I felt until he said "Time's up." Then I'd haul myself down to the bathroom, press my eyes with paper towels dipped in cold water, and walk slowly to my car.

We lived on the bottom floor of a house where our landlady, Mrs. Green, lived above us. By some quirk of plumbing, she controlled the heat to Keith's room and usually forgot to send it up. "No problem," she'd said when we signed the lease, and she'd repeat that on weekends, when I found her in the backyard leaning on a rake, a glass of scotch in her hand. "I don't know how I forget," she'd say with an unpleasant brown-toothed smile. "But I'll definitely remember starting tonight."

She wouldn't remember, and since she didn't answer her phone in the evening I'd tell Michael we should go up, bang on her door and make her keep her promise. He said that would just make things worse, to put an extra blanket on Keith. I knew he was right, but I was in no mood to let her get away with lying and forgetting us. But when I kept talking about confronting her, Michael would burrow deeper into his reading. He'd sit in his brown leather chair with his feet on a matching ottoman, by his side a small table holding a glass of white wine. I'd watch his long fingers turning the pages of some journal. Then I'd walk to the window and wonder how many of the cars passing through the fog had New York plates.

One afternoon before Christmas, I arrived home after a session with Dr. Alfred to find Mrs. Green sweeping leaves in front of the house. I asked her in, and when she sat down, I went on about the heat problem in Keith's room. She came back with something about our technically not being entitled to anything, and how what we got came out of a generosity that was quickly shrinking. I don't remember exactly what I said, but I jumped up and stood over her yelling, cursing, and threatening her with lawsuits and worse. Then she was at the door pulling a tan cardigan around her shoulders. "And you call yourself a psychiatrist," she said, laughing.

I felt humiliated. Except for fights with Michael, I'd prided myself on acting professional, controlled. Now I'd be known as Marjorie Raskin, the screaming psychiatrist. When would I explode next? As soon as Keith went to sleep, I told Michael what happened.

"Well, we should buy our own place," he said. "That way you'll be your own boss. At the hospital most couples our age are buying first houses. It makes good sense."

"But Michael, something's happening to me here. I'm having all these panics, and now this."

"You had panics in New York. You told me. And this was coming. Mrs. Green provoked you. She's a liar and a drunk."

"Michael, I'm in trouble."

"You'll be fine. We'll get our place when the lease is up. You'll pick it out. We can start looking now if you want." He smiled and went back to his reading.

I looked at Michael. I felt sad that I married a man who couldn't understand me. Yet that had drawn me to him. When Michael first proposed, I was pleased he didn't look far into my problems with loving or question what terrible flaws lay behind my panics, but in San Francisco with no one else to talk to, I felt alone. And a childish part of me blamed Michael for not being a god, for not making everything all right.

When I saw Doctor Alfred next, I sat opposite him and told him about the landlady. "I'm going out of control," I said. "Do something."

"But I am doing something. I'm analyzing you." He picked his pipe out of a thick glass ashtray and said, "Now, why don't you lie down and tell me what happened again, but go slow and let's see what comes to your mind."

"I'm not going back on that couch again. If this is all you can do, I've got to leave. I'm getting worse. Can't you see that?"

Dr. Alfred followed me to the door with a puzzled expression. "Call if you want to come back. You were making progress."

I wasn't.

When I left Dr. Alfred's office, I sat in my car for a long time. I thought back to when Philip stopped calling me and I'd felt dead inside. But now I knew that inside me was this vengeful, vicious creature that had to be kept out of sight while I smiled and acted nice, and above all, made myself useful so I'd have a place in the world.

"Get back in treatment," Richard urged again. I told him I'd wait a while. I tried to look at my case objectively, as a psychiatrist, but that only scared me more. I knew that some patients, sicker patients, often got worse with treatment. Was that my problem? I didn't know. I couldn't diagnosis myself objectively.

In my work with Ruesch I'd chosen to do my research on — what else? — anxiety. I started out by reading just about every scientific study on it written or translated into English. Since I'd had those panics over Philip eight years before, there'd been advances. Anxiety was seen as an entity in its own right, one that was often severe and chronic. The main view of its cause and treatment was analytic. From this perspective anxiety comes from hidden conflicts formed in childhood and reawakened by problems in our adult lives. Analytic therapies aim at uncovering and resolving these conflicts. This often works well for acute anxiety crises, but is less successful when the patient's anxiety is chronic. However, when it does work, many chronic patients stay well for years.

Ruesch wanted his fellows to do one actual study under his supervision. I wanted to study the effects of psychotherapy on chronic anxiety, but he said that was too complicated. Biofeedback for stress and tension was popular then, and it interested me. I started pilot work using muscle biofeedback to induce relaxation. Soon I got a small grant; later I got a big one.

Ruesch was pleased with my research activities, but often when we met, he'd end up telling me how upset I looked and asking what was wrong. He was a big man with broad shoulders, a full chest and large, bald head. With his composed expression and glittering gray eyes, he reminded me of a Caucasian Buddha. I desperately wanted to tell him how I felt, but was afraid to tell the one professor who'd given me a chance what I was really like inside.

Back in New York, Dr. Easser would tease me about not trusting doctors enough to let them treat me. "Are you going to deliver your own child?" she'd joke. But at this point I thought treating myself was best. I knew loneliness made me anxious, so I began making small dinners, inviting Michael's colleagues or mine. At one of them, I met Beth, a cardiologist's wife, who was going to live in

Minneapolis in a matter of weeks. She talked openly about her fears of moving to a new city, and I told her about my problems adjusting to San Francisco. Soon we were kidding around and agreeing we should've met sooner. A few days later she called, inviting Keith and me to brunch to meet her friend Amanda, a beautician, who had a boy, Billy, also two-and-a-half.

I felt hopeful as I sat sipping coffee at Beth's apartment in the Marina, Keith munching a chocolate chip cookie. A few minutes later the doorbell rang and Billy, a big boy with straight blond hair, strode into the room. When he saw Keith, his eyes grew wider, and he brought his hand to the side of his ruddy cheek. Keith had scrambled up on his knees and was looking at Billy over the back of the couch. The two boys stayed perfectly still except for their heads which they turned slowly toward each other, until that overwhelming moment of eye contact made them swiftly look away. They continued this for some time, their heads moving like animated figures in a store window.

Amanda stood in the doorway. Everything about her seemed ample and attractive — large, gold-flecked brown eyes, long, thick blond hair, full, smiling lips, solid flesh jammed into tight white jeans, overflowing breasts covered by a loose striped sweater. As she glided toward me, holding out a hand with long red nails, I wondered what we could possibly have in common. But I told myself to stop being a snob. In San Francisco I only knew doctors and doctor's wives, and that wasn't bringing me much comfort.

Amanda was funny, and seemed to like me. She said she'd had trouble making new friends here too. When she talked about Beth moving, she looked tearful. So did Beth. While Keith and Billy kept edging closer and smiling, Amanda and I exchanged phone numbers. As I left I said, "I'll call you soon."

"Why so formal." Amanda touched my hand. "Let's meet this Sunday at Julius Kahn. Say ten, ten-thirty?"

Julius Kahn was the big park in the Presidio with swings, a jungle gym, and a large ball field that doubled as a dog run. Behind it were groves of tall pines and eucalyptus. We met that Sunday, and the next, and the one after that. As the boys hiked through the woods fighting off imaginary snakes and dragons, Amanda and I talked. Mostly she talked about food. She'd go on about last night's roast, and how it was brown and crisp on the outside, and juicy and tender when she cut it. She told me she was separated and had just started back at work, but beyond that said little that was personal. I didn't mind; she was chatty and I liked being with her.

After some weeks, she said, "It must be fascinating to be a psychiatrist. You're probably great at understanding people."

I felt embarrassed and said, "I'm concentrating on research now."

A few days later, Amanda arrived at the park looking upset. We walked for a while, before settling under a huge pine tree to talk. After Billy's birth, her husband began staying out nights and weekends and eventually stopped giving her money. She tried to think about what to do and ended up crying in bed for days. Her parents came down from Oregon and took her to a psychiatrist who put her on anti-depressants. That was a year ago. She'd just come off her medication and was terrified she'd sink back into a depression. I put my arm around her shoulders and mostly listened.

Over the next weeks, I began confiding a little about my anxiety. One day I described a panic attack.

"Oh, that sounds awful," Amanda gasped. "If it happens again, call me — day or night."

I looked into her gold flecked eyes. She meant it.

Amanda and I began talking by phone in the evenings, after the boys were asleep. It was simple everyday talk, but it created a comfortable end to my day. Michael would come into the kitchen and frown. I'd smile but didn't rush to hang up. I was tired of looking at Michael's fingers on the back of his journals.

"Who's your fascinating new friend?" he'd ask. "When am I going to meet her?

I hesitated, knowing Michael would be put off by the way Amanda dressed and talked. But he kept pushing to meet this new person who took so much of my time.

When Amanda arrived for a Saturday lunch with Billy, Michael was peering out the front window. She wore a tight white sweater over even tighter white jeans. I'd told Michael that Amanda wore sexy clothes, but his nostrils dilated as if he smelled something foul.

In the hallway, he squatted down and talked to the boys, and his attention stayed on them through lunch. Amanda asked him a series of questions, but his answers to her were brief. "Yes, UC." "It's a great hospital." "No, I don't know him."

Amanda finished her salad, pushed her plate away, and studied Michael's face. "Capricorn, right?"

Michael flushed. "Lucky guess, or did Marge tell you?"

"Nobody told me anything. I can see it."

"You can see what?" Michael's face was stiff.

"That you're uncomfortable with feelings for one thing."

"That kind of talk is very California." Michael raked his hair back with his fingers.

"Who wants ice cream?" I asked in loud voice. The boys and Amanda did. Michael said he had to polish his car.

Amanda was long gone when Michael came back. "How can you spend time with her? She's a not a very nice person."

"You barely spoke to her. You don't even know her."

Michael looked at me with a confused expression, then shaking his head, picked up one of his journals.

Chapter 10. Filbert Street

Michael and I liked looking at mansions in Presidio Heights that were well beyond our means, as well as affordable homes throughout the city. We soon fell for a turn of the century house on Filbert Street, in a quiet neighborhood called Cow Hollow. It had been mostly pastures and orchards until the mid-1800s when private houses began squeezing out the farms. Our house, built as the last cow grazed, had a high peaked roof, peach-painted wooden siding, and a large sunny back garden.

Our first guests were Ray and Frieda Blum. Frieda, a psychiatrist, stood at the door, her thin body erect, her delicate face stunning with her dark hair newly cropped and feathered slightly at the back of her neck. When we'd first met, I kept Frieda at a distance because she seemed cold and controlling. But one afternoon in Chinatown with Keith, we bumped into Frieda and Ray with their four-year old daughter Melissa. Frieda insisted we go to her favorite restaurant where there was always a long wait. As we stood in the lobby, she lifted each child to the fish tank so they could see the glistening gold carp rise, gulping, to the surface. As the children opened their mouths imitating the fish, a warm smile spread across Frieda's face. I started to like her.

After giving the Blums a house tour, we sat in the back of the living room overlooking the garden, having champagne and paté.

Ray, a tall man with sleepy dark eyes and chiseled features, walked around rapping the walls with his knuckles.

"It's a great old house," he said, settling in beside Frieda. "Straight walls. Solid foundation. This baby will stand through the next big earthquake."

Frieda shook her head. "Don't say things like that. Most people don't like to think about earthquakes, especially us ex-New Yorkers."

"And this from a woman who makes her living helping people face the truth." Ray rubbed his wife's long neck until she moved her head forward and out of his reach. After a while, Ray and Michael got into to their usual discussion about who at the hospital was first rate this week. Ray was a top vascular surgeon at U.C., but so competitive that if another doctor's work was praised, he'd ask, "What about me?"

That afternoon Amanda had said, "See. It's all falling into place, just like I predicted." I thought about that, standing on our new stoop with Michael, the outside lights on, foghorns bleating below us.

By the time we moved to Filbert Street, I was less anxious. Occasionally I got dizzy or felt a tingling around my mouth, but these sensations didn't last. I was back in the world of people. Besides Ray and Frieda, there were the Douglasses, an agreeable couple whom I later discovered were usually stoned, and the Wangs who were nice, but formal. I spoke to or saw Amanda every day. She'd been good to Keith, and Michael had gradually warmed to her.

In our spare time, Michael and I worked with drop cloths and rollers coating the walls with Benjamin Moore White Linen. On the weekends Amanda helped out, mostly by watching Keith and Billy. At the end of the day, Michael barbecued in the backyard. We'd sit outside on those long September days, eating juicy hamburgers on grilled sesame buns.

When the painting was almost over, I began talking about having a second child.

"But I'm 37 years old," Michael said, pacing up and down in the den, raking his hair with his fingers. "I want to enjoy myself for a change. Do you really want to go through all that again?"

"I told you, I don't want Keith to be an only child. It's not good for him." I stood facing Michael, my arm on the back of a chair.

"But Keith is happy. Forget your problems, just look at him."

"Michael, this is important to me. You promised."

"I know, but what about my feelings?" Michael walked past me, through the kitchen, and out to the garden.

As I expected, Michael complained, but kept his promise. Alexis was born in March of 1971, about a year after we moved to Filbert Street. Amanda wanted to take Keith for an overnight when the baby was born, so he'd have special memories of that day. When I went into labor, which was gentle and slow, I packed Keith's overnight bag and called her. It was late morning, and as Michael turned onto Divisadero, the Bay sprung up before us, a long stretch of churning blue water topped with white sails. I passed that scene every day, but that morning I *saw* it.

Amanda and Billy were waiting in front of their building. Billy was bouncing a tennis ball, but when he saw Keith, he started jumping and shouting. Amanda held her arms open. The sun had turned her hair a pale gold color, and lit up one side of her face. She came to the car, touched the top of my belly, then lifted out Keith's bag. Michael got out, kissed Keith, and bent like he was going to kiss Amanda too. Instead he punched her gently on the arm.

"Are you Ok?" he asked me before speeding into a U-turn.

Alexis, born three weeks past her due date, looked like a tiny old person. Her face was deeply wrinkled, great bags pressed up against her eyes, and her overlong nails curled over her fingertips like little onion skins. Michael examined her in the delivery room, counted her fingers and toes, and declared her perfect.

When we came home two days later, Mom was there. A Welcome Home sign hung in the den, and popping through the round letters — the C's and O's — I saw the faces Keith had drawn. He kept peering at Alexis, hesitatingly touching her hand or foot. Mom cried with relief when she saw her. During both my pregnancies Mom was convinced the babies would be born deformed or retarded. Sometimes she'd call me from Brooklyn, sobbing. I didn't like listening to her, but I knew her awful predictions were less about me than her fear of God. It was as if worrying and crying and expecting the worst would appease him.

My mother stayed for ten days; my father spent the weekend. Mom, now retired, looked energetic and happy. From the moment she got up in the morning until she collapsed into bed at night, she was busy helping. She took over the cooking and bought new clothes for Keith. I saw her sit still only once each day. We had a black housekeeper, Dottie. Before Dottie left for the day, she and my mother sat at the kitchen table telling stories over tea. Most of my mother's were about me as a baby. How my grandma howled with laughter when I put my hands between my legs and yelled, "Hot piss." I liked hearing stories about grandma Golda, and I liked the warm sound of Mom's voice when she told them. I also felt an unexpected tenderness toward her when she'd sneak outside like a teenager, turn her back to the house, and stand smoking under the plum tree.

Our garden had a brick patio rimmed with blue lobelias, a copper-leafed plum tree, and along the fence, ancient rosebushes with large pink flowers. I nursed Alexis sitting on the patio in a beach chair, the sun warm on my legs. I'd take some reading out, but rarely got to it. Instead I held Alexis and watched her. She had smooth olive skin, pale fuzz on her head, and plump pink cheeks. In my off key voice I'd sing:

I don't want a pickle, just want to ride on my motorcycle.

And I don't want to die,

Just want to ride on my motorcyyy.

During the first few months of Ali's life, Michael wanted me to get babysitters so we could go out as usual, but it didn't really work. I'd be too tired or Ali too fussy. Michael was annoyed and tried acting as if Alexis didn't exist, but by the time she reached eight months, he could no longer resist her. If she gurgled, he rushed to pick her up. She made her needs known by gestures and sounds, and Michael would sit before her, trying to guess what she wanted and teach her words. Keith sat beside him, the second teacher. At first I was delighted, but soon realized this had a downside. When Keith was born, we'd become more of unit, but that hadn't happened again. When we went on family outings, Michael was preoccupied with the children — turning up the cuffs on their sweaters, checking their shoelaces, smoothing their hair. Glad to be back in shape again, I'd dress with care, but Michael didn't seem to notice. If I stopped to look in a shop window, he'd walk on until I called to him.

Once, after I'd spent the afternoon trailing after him, I said, "What's wrong? If you're angry at me, say so!"

"C'mon, we had a nice day. Don't spoil it."

"I had a terrible day. You ignored me."

"I didn't ignore you. I was busy with our children."

Michael looked annoyed and started to turn away. I stopped him with my hand. "You use those kids not to face me."

"Another great theory."

I hated to have Michael ignore me, but what bothered me even more was feeling jealous of the children, especially Alexis, not even one year old. Those feelings were unbearable. I wondered what I'd feel like when she was a beautiful teenager. A young woman. I didn't know exactly what was making Michael angry, but thought it was my not giving him enough attention. He didn't ask for attention, and when he didn't get it, he'd calmly go about his business. But I knew he had to be drawn out, asked how his day went, and listened to. Yet I didn't do much of that because I was busy, and angry about his neglect of me. Michael became increasingly calm while I grew needy and frantic. At times he called himself sane and mature, while he spoke of me as the childish, hysterical one. I knew I was angry but had no idea how truly furious I was.

One Sunday, I pulled into the Stonestown Shopping mall, seeking small pleasures for myself — maybe a new blouse or sweater. I saw a big banner announcing puppies for adoption. When I walked over to look, a bouncy gray puppy caught my eye. I walked over to his cage; he licked my hand through the grating. I debated whether to ask to hold him. He was begging, and looked so warm and loving.

Of course, bringing the puppy home like that was rotten. Once the kids saw him, he couldn't go back. Michael would be angry, and he'd be right. Yet I did it. The kids named him Arco, after the gas station. Michael stared at me, his upper lip drawn down in anger. "How the hell are you going to manage?" he asked.

I didn't know. I gave Dottie a raise so she'd help out more, but still it was over- whelming. I was working full-time, Alexis was in diapers, Keith was on the go, and the puppy needed training. Soon our house smelled of urine. Then when Arco was housebroken, which happened quickly because he was a smart little guy, I started to find teeth marks on the doors, the table legs, and the wall moldings. I sprayed each day with *Bitter Apple* and a pepper solution, but it made no difference.

Michael sat reading in his tan leather chair, acting as if he didn't notice the way the house was being gnawed, gnawed, gnawed to pieces. I worked to prevent the damage, but I have to admit it gave me pleasure. The house had been perfect looking, but that perfection was a lie. I was happy to see it go, and I enjoyed watching Michael struggling to stay calm. I was waiting for his outburst, but he found another way to get back at me.

Michael and I both worked in the garden, and sometimes we argued, because he liked a more manicured look. One Saturday afternoon I took Ali out in her stroller. When I got back every flower and shrub had been cut back so severely, the garden reminded me of a women shaved and prepped for an operation. I stood looking out the kitchen window, my fist jammed into my mouth to keep from screaming.

That evening we had plans with Frieda and Ray. We were going to see some spaghetti western that had gotten good reviews. I barely thought about the movie; I was wondering if Michael and I could act reasonable together. The theater was packed, so Michael and I sat in front, Frieda and Ray in back. The movie was bloodier than I expected, and as the deaths kept coming, I thought about leaving and turned to Michael. His expression was odd: frightened, yet startlingly alive. I kept watching him, his face lit by the screen. As each shot met its mark, he'd hold his belly, groan, and look even more excited.

When we were walking across the street to get coffee, Frieda and Ray behind us, I said, "You liked it."

"Of course. It's a good movie."

"How can you get pleasure from all those killings?"

"It's only a movie."

We were sitting with Ray and Frieda in a red leather booth, our coffees before us, along with plates of different kinds of pie. I told myself to keep quiet, but looking at Michael, said, "You get pleasure from causing pain."

"And you don't?"

Frieda was slowly eating her peach pie, watching us across the table.

"I kinda liked it too," Ray said with a smile.

Frieda's eyes stayed on us. "Maybe I'm out of line here," she said. "But I'm worried about you two. You are our best friends, and lately, you keep going at each other."

I felt embarrassed and looked at Michael, who was playing with his pie and blushing.

"We're in a kind of period of adjustment," he said, "There's a new baby and a new dog. Things'll settle down."

"But you keep making them worse," Frieda objected. "The dog, how did that happen?"

"Things happen," Michael said, in a close-the-subject tone.

I was pleased with him. I didn't like having this talk, and Michael was stopping it.

Frieda went back to eating her pie, occasionally looking up at us.

"A period of adjustment," Ray repeated. "Well, we have them too, only with ours, Frieda picks up Melissa and moves out."

Frieda stared at Ray.

Driving home, we speculated about what was happening with them. They didn't seem to speak the same language. Ray was always thinking about his work. They took good digs at each other. It sounded a lot like us, but we didn't seem to notice.

Back in the house I opened a bottle of Hearty Burgundy, and we sat drinking at the kitchen table. Arco was under my chair, his chin on my foot. He looked mostly like a Labrador, but with fluffy gray hair and large brown eyes. "I'm tired of all this fighting," Michael said, leaning back in his chair. "Let's call a truce."

"I'm tired of it too." I paused, then insisted, "But I do feel neglected."

"Well, we can fix that." Michael finished his wine. "Don't worry, we'll work out something."

We got a babysitter and went out on Saturday afternoons without the children. We walked around Fisherman's Wharf eating Crab Louie. We listened to street musicians at the Cannery, and browsed in Sausalito. We bought things for the house and the kids, and if I liked something for myself, Michael would insist we get it. He bought me a green fisherman's sweater from an Irish store because I admired it in the window. But still I knew that important things between us were missing.

Chapter 11. Close Supervision

I put flyers for my biofeedback studies around the medical center and got so many responses, I began thinking chronically anxious people filled the world. Medical students, nurses, administrators, lab technicians, secretaries kept calling in. When I interviewed them, I was struck by how often I heard disturbing stories about their childhood. A nurse with a psychotic mother was left alone for days as a child in Jamaica; she survived because neighbors fed her. As a punishment for wetting his pants, a research assistant was paraded through the streets dressed as a girl. Another subject, a doctoral candidate, received nightly beatings from drunken parents until he left home at sixteen. I began keeping track of these events in a systematic way and had a psychologist rate them. The individuals with panic level anxiety gave a history of gross neglect or abuse, while most with milder anxieties did not. How did these results fit with what Freud called the riddle of anxiety?

In his last major paper on anxiety — *Inhibitions, Symptoms, and Anxiety* — Freud asked why some individuals process anxiety as part of the normal workings of the mind, while others came to grief over it. This was a question I often asked myself. I wondered why I, and others like me, were the ones who came to grief. The person whose answers most satisfied me was the British psychoanalyst, John Bowlby.

Parent child interactions were Bowlby's lifelong interest. After World War II, the World Health Commission asked him to study the plight of children who had lost their parents and were living in foster care. His report contained the seeds of what would later be called Attachment Theory.

Bowlby considered attachment, not food, the child's most basic need. After thirty years of directing teams of therapists and researchers working with children and their families at the Tavistock Clinic in London, Bowlby claimed the single best predictor of whether an individual would be confident or anxious was how he was treated as a child. Like Freud, Bowlby emphasized an inner world that guided our feelings, and like Freud, he felt we often hid this inner world from ourselves. He believed that if a child learns to expect help when he needs and calls out for it, he carries that confidence into the world. He comes to view himself as worthwhile and expects friends and lovers to be responsive and protective. But if he has been neglected or abused like the panic patients in my study, his basic view of life is different — he sees himself as unworthy, and attachment figures as unavailable when needed, or even dangerous. In order to feel safe, he often creates false expectations. For example, he may idealize one or both parents, convincing himself they were always there to protect him. Such early distortions lead to later ones, so that friends or lovers are also idealized. Thus, the individual ends up with opposing sets of beliefs about himself and others — one set conscious and the other not. This leads to Panic in different ways. Acting on his idealized expectation, the individual may marry, or befriend someone, only to have his hopes repeatedly shattered. Finding himself hurt and disappointed, his rosy beliefs fall away, allowing him a glimpse of his more basic and terrifying views; views that often cause panic. Other individuals may follow their false expectations, but like me planning to marry Philip, discover their hidden views keep signaling overwhelming dangers that they can't understand.

I was excited about my research findings. They added to our knowledge and gave me insight into my own panics. Michael was pleased I had reportable findings, but he had his own view of how childhood traumas affected adult behavior. He believed the early problems you got through, made you stronger. I tried to believe that about myself as well. But with me it was different; I had painful, almost crippling symptoms, while in most ways, Michael's life was a major success.

When I told Ruesch about my findings, he asked me to present them at Grand Rounds, the major weekly teaching conference for the department. I made slides, wrote and rewrote my presentation, and rehearsed in front of Michael until my words sounded smooth. I was slightly nervous as I looked out at my large audience, but as soon as I began talking I felt better. What I remember most about that day was how elated I felt standing on stage in my periwinkle blue dress, talking and taking questions.

I think because my lecture went so well, I was asked to run an outpatient team. That was a job I'd wanted from the beginning. With the help of another psychiatrist, I was ultimately responsible for the work of about twenty-five people including social workers and psychiatric residents. I ran teaching conferences for my team, as well as conferences about whom to accept for treatment and whom to discharge. I liked the group teaching and supervising the residents, and did it well.

In January, a second year resident, Jeffrey Walter Hansen, joined my team. Walt was a broad-shouldered Texan with fine brown hair and passionate dark eyes. He was bright and idealistic, always arguing to have every patient seen two or three times a week. When he first arrived in my office for supervision, I thought he'd keep arguing, but he looked quietly at the picture on my desk — one with the kids, Michael and Arco— and said, "You must be very proud of them." After I nodded, he asked if I wanted to see pictures of his family. He showed me a snapshot of his wife, a pretty blonde. His smile wider, he handed me a picture of himself sitting in his red Triumph convertible beside Murph, his Irish setter. I was thinking that was odd when he said, "Oh, I'm in analysis."

Walt was conscientious and talented, and supervising him went well. Usually, I had little to add, but when I did, he was full of compliments.

"That's exactly right, that is what she meant. I see it now."

After some weeks, he sat closer to me, and when we spoke, his hand sometimes grazed my arm. I knew I should say something, but didn't.

March started with cold, damp weather. Walt moved even closer, and his compliments grew more personal. They had an edge.

"You're attractive, very attractive, but sort of … well, uptight."

"For someone so attractive, you give off this stay-away vibe. Look at your hair. Those bobby pins are like thorns. Do you want to seem so untouchable?"

"Your suits are nice, but they hide your body. You look like you're wrapped in layers and layers of cloth." His hands circled mine as if mimicking the wrapping.

On a cool morning in mid-March Walt arrived at my office in high spirits, carrying two hot chocolates. "You know, I could help you," he said. "I'm good at getting people to relax. I'm sort of an unwrapper." Before leaving, he leaned over me and whispered, "Think it over."

After he was gone, I was filled with vivid sensations of Walt's body against mine. That afternoon I left early, drove to the Presidio, and parked at a lookout. Fog was forming over the bay, wiping out the landmarks. Marin was gone, and the Golden Gate Bridge was disappearing in a mass of clouds. It was 1972 — still the sixties in San Francisco — where a major aim was expanding your mind through experiencing everything from drug-induced hallucinations to orgies. I'd seen lots of friends go from affairs, to open marriages, to divorces, and didn't want to travel that route. I had to get myself under control, and the best way, I thought, was to tell Michael. I'd just treated a medical student who'd rushed into treatment after discovering his wife was having an affair. The affair turned out to be his wife's method of getting the attention of her preoccupied spouse. At least I'd be telling Michael before anything happened. I drove home quickly, convincing myself this was the right move.

Michael was in the den, reading. He looked up and said a quick hello.

I sat on a footstool.

He closed his book, keeping his place with his finger. "What's up?"

"I think we should talk — about us."

Michael's face stiffened. "Okay, I'm listening."

I looked at Michael and knew going on would just get him angry. "It's nothing," I said. I looked out at the garden. It needed work, but I felt tired.

Chapter 12. Carmel

Standing on the corner behind the hospital, waiting for Walt to pick me up in his shiny red Triumph, I felt crazy. Why was I risking so much for a couple of hours in a strange apartment with a married man ten years my junior who promised me nothing?

I'd get back to the hospital, usually in time for a research meeting, the skin around my lips chafed red, stray hairs falling in my face, my French twist sitting at an angle at the back of my head, thinking everyone here must know or suspect. The talk in the room whizzed by me as possible consequences of being caught with a resident bubbled up in my mind. And once I began worrying about losing my job, worries about losing my marriage followed. When I drove off with Walt, I wore a scarf, dark glasses, and kept the top down, but still my own husband would know me. I thought if Michael found out, pride alone would make him go.

But worrying didn't stop me from waiting on that corner week after week. Our affair had started in July of 1972, after Walt left my team, and just kept going. In the fall, I began driving up to the hospital on the nights Walt was working, telling Michael I had to use the computer center. Computers were the size of large rooms then, and we fed in stacks of punch cards that sometimes got stuck. The whole staff of the Psychiatric Hospital used this one center, and I often did work there in the middle of the night.

On those evenings, I'd shower, slowly rub my body with a Freesia-scented lotion, put on black silk underwear, slacks, a sweater, lipstick, blush, and maybe a string of pearls. It pleased me to see myself in the full-length bedroom mirror: I hadn't looked that attractive in years. I knew it was mostly because I felt happy, but I did look slightly different. My hair was cut to shoulder length, and I was picking better fitting clothes. It felt sexy when the soft wool of my sweater or the lining of my slacks rubbed against my skin. I thought I radiated a sensuousness so palpable anyone could feel it. Before going downstairs, I'd put on a jacket. Michael would barely look at me, as I hurried out feeling guilty.

It was almost a half-hour drive to the hospital, and as I drove, going quickly with one hand on the wheel, I had the odd, but not unpleasant, feeling that I could simply rise into the air like some exotic kite.

Walt would open the on-call room door, an excited smile on his face. We'd kiss and talk and make love. And always, when we talked we touched. He liked pressing my foot with both of his and stretching so our bodies came together from shoulder to toe. I told him how, as a child, I'd pictured heaven as a balcony filled with old Jewish women. My grandma Golda would be up front in a flowered housecoat, and whenever I did something wrong, the other women would rub one index finger across the other to shame her. Walt had no childhood pictures of heaven, but vivid ones of a flaming hell.

He talked a lot about his difficulty loving Holly, saying he was in treatment to open up to her more. He'd had other affairs, and he and Holly had separated once. I took all that as a sign that his marriage was failing. He never said he loved me, but I felt he did. We worked in different buildings, and he was constantly coming by to say hello. Sometimes he'd sit in his car at Julius Kahn, watching me with my kids. We got together whenever we could, and I could always feel him yearning for more.

Amanda often asked what Walt meant to me. Did we have a future? I'd say it's out of the question, but I was up to my eyeballs in fantasies about him. I'd picture us walking arm in arm through the Presidio, my children with us, and Arco and Murph trotting in front, their long tails wagging. I could see us all traveling across the country, taking the kids to cookouts and fairs, but the image of us living in one house was murky. I focused on our age difference as the problem. I was approaching forty and thought, in the not too distant future, I'd lose all my appeal. I read that facelifts could take off about ten years, but they had to be repeated, and you could end up with a weird over-stretched look. Walt would laugh about these worries and tell me I'd always be attractive.

When he graduated from the residency program the following June, at least the danger of losing my job was over. With that change, I hoped that his marital situation would change too. It didn't. I kept on meeting him, regularly but not as often, and he seemed a cooler. He said he was busy working part-time and building a practice, but I felt he was losing interest. Then there was an incident that really upset me. Right after the Yom Kippur War, the Arab League staged an oil boycott to punish Israel's allies, sending gas prices sky high. We had rationing, and getting gas took hours. Walt bragged that he had a secret station with no waiting. When I asked where, he wouldn't tell. Finally he gave me the name, but I was hurt. No real lover would act like that.

I was always uncomfortable being between two men, but as my romantic fantasies about Walt faded, I began to feel sleazy. I planned to break off with him so I could be clear about my marriage, but sensing two losses to come, I was in no hurry to act. I'd watch the holidays go by — Labor Day, Thanksgiving, Christmas. I kept floating, balancing my marriage by seeing Walt.

Frieda called late in the morning on New Years' Day, 1974. We were having breakfast, and I wiped maple syrup from my hand to take the phone.

"We did it," she said.

"You did what?"

"Ray and I, we separated."

"What!"

"He got his own place. Look, Ray wants to be famous, and he doesn't have time for me."

"But, he was always ambitious."

"It's different now. He's got a nurse up at the hospital who'll gladly wait around while he makes his mark."

"He's having an affair?"

"That's the least of it. He thinks I can be replaced by someone less demanding, and if he finds me so easy to replace, then I want out while I can still replace him. You understand."

"Of course."

"I'm sorry, Frieda"

"Don't be. I'm not."

I hung up feeling surprised and confused. Michael, on his way out with Keith, said he'd believe it when he saw it. Ali was sitting in her special plastic chair, her back to the window, eating a sausage. I got another cup of coffee and sat across from her as she waved her sausage, saying "Goot, Goot." I smiled and said "good" back, but felt two-faced talking in this cheerful everyday way with her, while thinking about Frieda's decision. I was upset that Frieda's family was breaking up, but partly pleased. Now my future didn't look so bleak.

Frieda and Ray got together on and off for months. Then it seemed over. When I visited Frieda and her daughter Melissa would be there, I'd bring my kids. Melissa was quieter, and she'd hold Frieda's hand or sit on her lap. Frieda only let her sadness show when we were alone. Slowly, she moved into the dating scene. She complained of feeling lonely, although she attracted men easily. One weekend she asked me to go with her to Tahoe on a ski weekend. She wanted company. I was curious, and Michael agreed. Frieda was a good skier, and during the day she went off on her own. It was beautiful and quiet, and I spent a lot of time walking around, looking at the blue-white fields of ice crusted snow. I was content to walk and enjoy the silence. In the evenings, after Frieda and I had dinner, we'd sit in the lodge by the fire, and a few men would join us. Twice, I went for a walk down the snow-covered road in front of the lodge, listening to a man tell me the story of his divorce — what led to it, and how it hurt and surprised him. Both these men were polite and friendly and waited to see if I had a story too. Driving back on Monday, Frieda and I taking turns at the wheel, I thought to myself it was a reassuring weekend. Maybe I could handle being single.

When I got home it was late, and Michael was standing in the kitchen, his upper lip drawn down. I was hungry, got chicken from the refrigerator, and took it to the table.

Michael watched me, sighing and raking back his hair.

"You shouldn't spend so much time with Frieda," he said abruptly. "She wants you to join her. She's changing you."

I wiped my fingers on a paper napkin and looked up at him. "It's not her. It's us." I paused, wondering if I should continue. "Michael, I'm not happy. I don't think we're happy together."

"I'm happy." Michael stood taller. "The problem is you. I look outside and see it's sunny. You look out and ask yourself if it feels sunny. Everything with you is feelings, feelings, feelings. How you felt when you were five determines if you think it's nice today. No one can live like that."

"Everyone's world is colored by how they feel. It's a fact of life." I looked at the chicken, but my appetite was gone.

"I'm talking degree, and you know it. You and your psychiatric buddies spend all your time reaching inside, trying to fix your little egos. And it's a pity, because it doesn't work. You're going to spend your whole life pissing into the wind."

Michael seemed pleased and smug, and worst of all maybe right. I put the chicken back and turned to him. I looked at his high bridged nose, the confident set of his mouth, the contempt in his eyes. I had to wipe that expression off his face.

"I don't need to hear this. I had a good time. You're dragging me down. Maybe Ray and Frieda had the right idea. Maybe we should try a separation."

I hadn't meant to say it, but once the words were out of my mouth, they took on a life. They fluttered around the house, and when Michael and I quarreled, they were there whether we said them or not. And the longer they stayed, the more they changed us. I watched the idea of a separation go from possible to probable, and didn't even know if that's what I wanted.

I'd read books by Ashley Waters, a San Francisco analyst, on change and inner healing. He was a renegade Freudian who emphasized action. I liked his ideas, and called for an appointment.

The evening I went to see him it was storming. Rain came in huge sideways blasts; lightning slashed the darkness. His office was in a large room on the second floor of his house. It was lined with bookcases and sparsely furnished with Mission pieces in dark oak, making the room look like a monk's cell. Ashley himself added to that ascetic look. He was gaunt and pale, with sad blue eyes, and a precise mouth that covered long protruding teeth. It must've been a hard face to have as a child.

Speaking across oceans of worn Persian carpet, I told him about my affair, my marriage, my trouble making a decision.

"The affair, is it serious?" he asked, an intense look on his face.

I sat thinking for a moment. "No. We don't love each other." I'd known that, but saying it out loud gave it a stronger sense of truth.

The wind blew fiercely making the frames rattle, but Ashley paid no attention. "And your marriage? Tell me about that."

I talked about feeling unhappy and neglected. But said that Michael was a good person — a good father — that I didn't know what I felt about him anymore.

"So, you have a lot to sort through." Ashley nodded his head in a sympathetic manner. He asked about the children. When I described Keith and Ali he smiled, and as I kept talking about them, his face warmed so much that he began to seem like a doting grandparent. I looked around his office for pictures of his family, but saw only Ansel Adams photographs of Yosemite. When Ashley asked about my background, I told him about my panics and different treatments. He made notes and nodded. But when I talked about Yollie, he looked concerned, upset really, and rubbed his fingers across his lips. I felt he understood me, and agreed to come weekly.

At Grand Rounds that week, the speaker was Joe Wheelwright, one of the main teachers at the Jungian Institute in San Francisco. He started out saying he'd gone into psychiatry to save himself and thought most therapists did that. This was not a new idea, but it was rarely stated so openly. It made me feel better. Certainly I'd done it. I was sure Ashley had too. And as a patient the idea didn't frighten me.

In fact I always thought therapists who had experienced emotional pain made better contact with their patients. The therapists who scared me were the ones who didn't seem to have any problems, or thought they didn't, and looked at patients as another kind of person. I thought Dr. Alfred fit into that group. By then I'd realized that he'd made a major treatment mistake: he couldn't adapt his analytic style to me, his patient.

I had sessions with Ashley regularly for almost a year, and I'd swing from thinking my marriage could work to feeling it was impossible. My relationship with Michael mirrored those swings. Sometime I'd look at him, see our children's eyes in his, and feel I do love him. Or he'd be funny, and I'd think how much I'd miss him. Or I'd watch him with the children and decide we're a unit, we have to stay together.

But other times I'd feel certain our marriage had to end. I felt it most when Michael ignored me, and I felt jealous of Ali. I also felt it when I was trying to talk to him about being worried, or lonely, or concerned about the children, and he'd brush me off saying I always worried.

Other women's attitudes affected me too. With Frieda, who had a way of being interested in things and happy, I felt I could make it. But when I was around sad divorced women, I'd get more fearful. Amanda had tried to build her life around work and Billy, but ended up in painful affairs with married men. Most other divorced women I met were bitter and lonely, resenting how quickly their ex-husbands had found new partners.

Even though my relationship with Michael was going through all these back- and-forth swings, there was a steady overall movement toward parting. I could feel it. I guess Michael did too. One afternoon I came home to find pink roses on the mantle and Michael waiting in the den.

"Look," he said. "Let's not rush into anything. Let's take a long weekend and go to Carmel. You always liked it there."

We hadn't been away without the kids for years. The suggestion made me nervous, but I made reservations at a motel we'd liked.

It was May and Carmel had perfect weather — sunny days and cool clear nights. The motel looked better than it had a few years before when we'd stayed there with the kids. The jade plants in front had grown big as trees.

The first morning we poked into little shops with work by local artists. We bought carved animals for Ali who had a collection (she was never big on dolls), and books and puzzles for Keith. At sunset, we stood on the beach with our arms around each other, but as the sky grew radiant with pinks and reds, our arms slipped to our sides. We went to a new restaurant with a big glass window and shiny brass poles and found ourselves with little to say besides "How's your salmon?" "Good, your steak?" The last night we made love. It was tender, and afterwards we sat on opposite sides of the bed, looking at the floor. Michael seemed sad. I wanted to say something about his sadness, a sadness I felt too. But I thought he'd get angry, tell me I was crazy, that he didn't feel sad at all.

I looked at Michael's face, and thought his sadness had been there since I met him. That sadness, one I couldn't talk about, along with mine, seemed more than I could handle. I knew the marriage was over. I don't know what Michael thought, but driving back the next day he said, "Look, we can stay together and live separate lives. I'd prefer it, and it's better for the kids. Or, I can start looking for an apartment. Just remember your Ashley Waters didn't do us any favor."

Chapter 13. Single in San Francisco

Before Michael left, I sat each child down to explain what was happening. Keith was in bed wearing his red plaid pajamas. Almost nine, he was a serious boy, with a streak of humor that could make me helpless with laughter. He sat quietly, looking at the walls he'd covered with meticulous drawings of his superheroes — Thor, Spiderman, Captain America, The Incredible Hulk.

"All right," he said in a subdued voice, "But, I wanna be able to walk to Dad's on my own."

I nodded. I ached to hug him but that wasn't always welcome. I placed my hand between his shoulder blades where the round bones of his spine poked out. He didn't pull away, but he didn't move toward me either. We sat like that for a while, then he looked down at his pillow.

Ali, who was just over three, stared at me as if my words made no sense. She stared that same way every time I said her father would be living in another apartment. Michael and I agreed it was best for him to move while the children were at school. When Ali came back to a half-empty house, she rushed to her room, found the pacifier she hadn't used in months, and stuck it in her mouth. I kept giving her explanations. Michael took her to his apartment, but at home she walked around looking bewildered, the pink pacifier working in her mouth.

She went back to a time when she clung to me. At her nursery school, I literally handed her to Cindy, her favorite teacher, and drove off while she cried. I'd call from work to hear she was playing. That helped. She was with me once when I tried to leave Arco at the Vet overnight for worming, something we'd done before, but as soon as he disappeared down the hall, she sat down on the floor and cried until I got him back. Later, I held her on my lap and stroked her hair. Words meant so little to her then. I worried about the kind of unspoken beliefs she was forming.

I thought both children looked sadder, and Keith's way of leaving the house changed too. Michael had moved three blocks away, and Keith often visited him. When he went, he walked out the door as if there were blinders beside his eyes, and never once looked back. I didn't have words that could help. He had to do something hard, and he had to do it on his own. I knew it was important to stay civil with Michael when the children were around, and after one ugly scene that made them cry, we managed it.

Two weeks after Michael left, my panics came back. At first they left me dizzy and queasy for hours. I felt best late in the evening when the children were in bed and I sat in the den with Arco watching sitcoms like *Mary Hartman, Mary Hartman*. Work, friends, and home when the children were there, were safe havens, and I felt like I was lurching from one haven to the next. Weekends alone were the hardest. I'd try to spend some time with Frieda or Amanda then. One Saturday Frieda was over and we browsed in stores on Union Street. I was dizzy but tried to hide it. Back at my house, Frieda asked me how I was. I answered truthfully, and she grew so alarmed, she wanted to drive me either to Ashley's office or a Psych ER. I said no, and immediately acted as if I were better. But her response confirmed my fear of being terribly sick.

Ashley helped get me through those first months. He said that the more I pushed myself to do what I had to, the better off I was; he reminded me of all I'd done despite being anxious. He stayed reassuring when my anxiety spilled into new places. I began having panics while driving over bridges. With my anxiety level so high, natural dangers like heights which had never bothered me before were sufficient to cause terror. I hated driving where I felt so anxious but couldn't avoid it. I'd go slowly, nibbling a Valium, and praying for a traffic jam. Once, when I was crawling along on the Bay Bridge, a traffic officer came over to be sure I was all right, making Keith feel humiliated. When Michael had the children for the weekend, I sometimes practiced going across the bridges. Practicing helped, but not enough to get me comfortable.

I worked hard to look confident and happy, flashing false smiles I hoped fooled the children. It wasn't a great solution, but even now I can't think of a better one. When I was growing up, my mother's terrors kept flooding into me, and I didn't understand it. Probably I would've felt better if at some point she could have talked about being anxious. But confessing my problems to my small children felt wrong, like shifting the burden. The only good solution I could imagine was to try to feel well, and sometimes I succeeded.

I was pleased when my parents came out to visit. It was comforting to see my father's *New York Times* lying around the living room, and so was the smell of cigarette smoke that drifted after my mother.

Ever since I'd started talking about a separation, Mom was supportive. She'd say, "I'm glad you're doing something now. He's not going to change." She resumed her kitchen table talks with Dottie, but now they were about how the children and I were really doing. She went through the children's closets, mended their clothes, and bought them new outfits. She went through my closet too, and wanted to take me shopping. That would make me feel too much like a child so I didn't go. But I loved having her fuss over me. I craved it.

By now I had a better picture of my mom. It was only in recent years that she could talk about her mother without crying. Golda, who had no family here, had come from Latvia with a young female cousin. In New York, she worked in a grocery store and married a handsome man with a sweeping mustache who turned out to be a womanizer and gambler and eventually left her. Golda became my mother's best friend and only family. I'm not sure that explains why my mother's extreme grief lasted so long, but I also knew there was no point questioning her about the past. She only told me what she wanted to, and perhaps that's all she saw.

A couple of nights before my parents left, Michael had the children for the evening. When Keith came back, he said they'd been to dinner with a blond woman they'd been out with before. Mom's eyes widened, and her lips grew pale. My father was out walking. I put the kids to bed and went back down to her.

"He's going to remarry," she cried, flakes of tissue falling from her hand. "He'll have a whole new family. He'll forget you and the children. You'll have nothing. NOTHING!"

I felt scared, but my brain flashed messages saying this is crazy. And it was crazy. I was a doctor with excellent credentials. Michael and I made almost the same amount of money. I was the only child of a generous father who was a full partner in a prosperous law firm. But did I say any of that to my mother? No. I sat listening in terror, agreeing with her every word. My father came in, listened for a minute, and said, "Lilly, please. You're talking nonsense." My mother wiped her eyes, relaxed, and smiled. I relaxed too.

It was a strange moment. It had been clear for years that my mother could build a tragic world out of almost nothing. It was also clear that I could do exactly the same thing. But it was the first time I realized that it took a confident voice like my father's to bring me to my senses. No wonder I always had to have a man around, a competent one at that. I told Ashley we had to work on this. He nodded and made a note. Agenda item two hundred and seventy something.

Soon after my parents left, Richard, the psychiatrist who'd been Ruesch's other fellow, and his wife Sarah, asked me and the children to lunch. They had a new house in Berkeley where Richard now worked. I'd met Sarah at a few hospital functions and liked her.

By the time I made it over the Bay Bridge, I was wiped out. Sarah answered the door and hugged each of us. It was a tight hug, and I could feel the warmth of her cheek and smell lemon on her hands. She was young, about thirty, with clear blue eyes, high color, and curly dark hair. With her heavy leather sandals and white satin blouse over a tie-dyed cotton skirt, she looked like a cross between an orthodox Jew and a hippie.

She led us to the kitchen where Richard sat at the table with Rachel, their infant daughter. Rachel was in a high chair, laughing. Ali was smitten with this gleeful infant. She sat beside her, handing her rag dolls, pot-holders, bibs, all of which Rachel threw right down, screaming in delight.

Richard, showing a new side of himself, talked with Keith about comics. As we sat together, talking, drinking juice, and eating cheese and crackers, I felt a deep comfort. Sarah wanted to show me around the house. I got up, surprised to hear no protests from Ali.

The house had big shady rooms and exposed redwood beams. Glass jars holding cuttings and rooting avocados pits lined the windowsills. As we walked around upstairs, Sarah said she'd heard a lot about me from Richard and was glad we were finally getting together like this. She talked a little about Richard's work at a clinic in Berkeley, and how, after she raised a family, she wanted a career, maybe as a therapist. She was good with people, and I encouraged her.

As we started downstairs, Sarah took my hand and looked into my eyes. "If I'd chosen to be worldly, I'd be just like you," she said. "And if you worked on your spirit, you'd be like me. So, you see, we're like sisters."

I wasn't used to such talk, or having an adult woman hold my hand. I stepped back, wondering if she was a flake.

"Oh, you're shy," she said, smiling gently. At that moment I felt that she was much older than I was.

At lunch, there was a lot of talking and laughter, and when it was time to go, all three of us had difficulty leaving.

After that, Sarah often invited us to her house for Friday night dinners. She taught Ali to light the *shabbos* candles. I found myself watching the way Richard and Sarah spoke and touched each other. Once, while we were talking, a dab of sour cream clung to Richard's lower lip. I was about to tell him, when Sarah reached across the table and wiped it off with her finger. That gesture stuck with me.

When dinner didn't work out, Richard and Sarah called Fridays before sundown to wish us a good *Shabbos*. Each of them would get on a different extension, and it felt more like a visit than a call.

As 1975, my first year without Michael, came to a close, I wanted to do something for Rosh ha-Shana. Sarah had invited us over, but that would mean a long evening with two trips over the bridge. Instead, Frieda and I decided to make dinner at her house. We invited Amanda and Billy. The meal went well, and at the end, we dipped slices of apple in honey. As Frieda and I lingered by ourselves at the table, the candlelight showed a wistful expression.

"Special New Years thoughts?" I asked.

"I just wonder why I stay here. My family's in New York, and so are most of my friends. And the men I'm meeting here are either married, gay, or have five girlfriends."

"Are you seriously thinking about moving?"

"I don't know. I don't know how Melissa would feel. I don't know what Ray would do. I'll be here next New Year."

"Good." I sat at the table, breathing deeply.

That night I drove home slowly, feeling edgy.

I was glad to go back to work. Seated in front of my team, I felt nervous until we were underway. I felt confident while supervising my residents and later when I saw patients. They talked about their shame, loneliness, neediness, or rage, and I'd be impressed by their decency or courage and feel something like love for them.

Work buoyed me in other ways. After I'd separated from Michael, I started having lunch with a group of researchers who ate together in the third floor conference room. Notch, the head of research, was always there. So was an Indian post-doc, Deva Ponchali. He'd just gotten a Ph.D. in psychology from Berkeley and did research for Notch. I'd watch him perched on a stool in the lunchroom, laughing and clapping his pink-palmed hands, thinking he looked like an Indian prince. His dark eyes blended with his pupils, and his teeth gleamed white against his skin. Whenever he saw me, he smiled and made a point of taking me aside each day to ask how I was.

"Separations are so delicate," he'd say. "How are ya? And how are kiddoes?"

I'd answer, wondering if he was being polite or interested in me. He told me a little about his life in India and his work with Notch, but despite all my fishing I didn't have a clue if he was married, or living with someone, or had a house full of kids.

"Is it lonely being so far from your family?"

"No, I have friends here now."

"Your lunch looked so good. Who cooked it?"

"I should've have given you a taste. It was *Muttar Panir* — peas and Indian cheese."

He'd smile, fling his black and beige plaid jacket over his shoulder, and leave me to breath in the mixture of cinnamon, cumin, and clove that rolled off his body like fog from the ocean.

Chapter 14. Between Panics

Ali jumped into my arms and sprinkled my face with kisses. I saw the edge of her snub nose, a wedge of round cheek, and smelled peanut butter breath. Dottie fished in her purse for her keys; Keith pulled on his jacket. We were going to the park even though I'd just run a two hour suicide review while fighting down a panic.

Driving back, a headache started.

"Kentucky fried chicken."

"No, McDonald's!"

Their words landed like a hammer on my skull.

"Kids, quiet down. Please. You know I don't like screaming."

"Chicken with Biscuits."

"A Cheeseburger."

"I'll pick up both. Just be quiet."

Silence.

Giggles.

"Keith pinched me."

"She kicked me."

"OOOuch."

My head was nearly exploding, and the kids jumping blocked my view out the back window. *All right, Marjorie, keep yourself under control. Pull off to the side and speak softly, but with authority. You can do it.*

I missed a stop sign, saw a car coming, but swerved just in time. Breathing deeply, I parked by the curb. I looked through closed eyes at a patchy red darkness. I didn't want to speak until my heart slowed down.

"Okay, kids. This is dangerous. You have to stay in your seats and be quiet. Keith, I'm counting on you. No matter what happens stay in your seat and be quiet."

I released the emergency brake. Keith, laughing, did a pratfall against the front seat.

I turned and slapped him full in the face.

Tears filled Ali's startled eyes. Keith's face turned into a twisted mask of hurt and rage. I wanted my right hand to fall off. I wanted to reel back the moment.

"I'm sorry. I'm sorry, I'm sorry. This will never happen again. I promise"

The children stared ahead as if they didn't know me. I barely knew myself. Then I thought about my fight with our landlady in Pacific Heights, the times I wanted to kill my mother. It was *me* all right, the *me* I wanted to forget.

When I told Ashley about the slap, he winced and sat back in his chair. I felt hollow and evil.

He gave me rules. I was to keep track of my feelings and take a Valium as soon as I felt panicky, but that didn't work out. My panics lasted about thirty minutes, but after they left, the Valium made me groggy for hours. Instead we agreed I'd take time out. I had to write reports about each day with the children and read them in session. He also made short speeches, "You're stronger than you think. Each new behavior creates change." I felt he was distant, maybe doing some kind of crisis intervention for a while.

A couple of weeks later he said, "Well, we've reached our goal. Of course you can always call if problems come up."

"I don't understand. What goal? I came here to straighten out my life."

A pink blush spread across his face. "Look, you're doing better with your children. You've made important decisions about your life. I can't take you further. It's not your fault, but we're just too different."

I stared at him, unable to understand his words.

He sighed. "It's hard to explain. You see, I'm a gentle person with the temperament of, well, a Golden Retriever, but you, you're more the German Shepherd."

Driving back I felt hopeless. What was wrong with me anyway? I had all this leftover rage from childhood. Was that it? I'd been told I had too little trust, but that didn't feel right. If anything, I trusted too much. I trusted Alfred then Ashley, and they weren't worth trusting. And then there was the issue of my blindness to myself. How did that fit in? It was awful, knowing I couldn't see what was wrong with me.

I hadn't told Deva about my anxiety for fear of frightening him off, but after my treatment ended I blurted everything out.

"How can you be upset by that man," Deva said, laughing. "He's the one with problems. Listen to how he speaks — he's a Golden Retriever, you're a German Shepherd. Did he study psychology at veterinary school?"

I bent over laughing. Deva was laughing too. When I stood there with him, I felt normal.

"Everyone has panics at times," Deva said. "When I first got to the U.S., I didn't know anyone. I didn't have much English. I'd walk down a block and sometimes think the buildings would topple over on me. It went away. You're under a lot of pressure, bringing up two kids on your own." He moved closer. "If a kid cries in my family, my sisters come running, so does my mother, and if they're not around my brothers step in. India has its problems, but at least there they know people weren't meant to be alone."

I studied Deva's face as he looked at mine. The skin below his eyes was dark and finely wrinkled, his cheeks shown like polished wood, and his lips were smooth, a lilac color.

After the kids were asleep I draped a silk scarf of peacock blue around my head, put on long gold earrings, darkened my lids with a soft black pencil and looked at myself in the mirror, trying to picture myself as an Indian bride. I longed for a honey-skinned baby with big black eyes

I read *The Raj Quartet, Passage to India,* and *Heat and Dust.* I saw the films of Satyajit Ray. I wandered through the Indian groceries in Berkeley inhaling those incredible smells, then bought a book on Indian cooking. After browsing through it, I threw out my bottle of curry powder and stocked my shelves with cumin, turmeric, saffron, cardamom, cinnamon sticks, and coriander. I made curried shrimp and *tandoori* chicken, seared vegetables in mustard seeds that popped black from the pan. I made cool *raita,* and hot spiced tea. I began inviting Frieda and Melissa and Amanda and Billy to my Indian feasts. Deva kept asking how I was, but that's all he asked.

"I just don't understand him," I said to Frieda. "He cares. So why doesn't he make a move or tell me why he can't?"

We were in Frieda's back yard, sitting in lounge chairs with thin white plastic straps. Melissa was painting Ali's toenails geranium red.

"I told you, you have to be more aggressive," Frieda said, looking down at her own tanned toes. "Ask him to dinner or a movie. If he says no he has to give you a reason."

Ali and Melissa ran inside.

"But that could be embarrassing. I see him every day."

Frieda held bottles of different colored polish against her feet. "You don't want to end up waiting for nothing."

I pointed to the red I thought looked best. "Well, waiting isn't all that bad. I have someone to dress up for. I make great plans in my head. If he said no, I might get even more panics. I couldn't handle that."

Frieda looked up. "I'm sorry. Sometimes I forget."

The recent attacks had changed me. I lived in my own bubble. It was a prison and a protection. Anxiety simplified my world; it was part of my every decision. I was eager to remarry yet had no guilt about not going out of my way to meet men. When I left the house each morning, walked down the halls in the hospital, entered a conference room or library, I worried whether a panic would hit, and often it did. Just getting through the day was a triumph.

I'd been separated well over a year when Deva said we had to talk. It was the end of summer, and people were coming back with their vacation pictures. He followed me to my office and sat stiffly in a chair, his hands on his knees.

"I'll be away for most of September," he said. "I wanted you to know that."

I nodded.

"I've been living with a woman, Susan, for some time now." He stopped and looked at me. "It hasn't been working well. The last few years, we've been like brother and sister. On this vacation I'm going to talk things out with her. I care for her, so I want to do it right."

Deva looked nervous. I smiled, and he smiled back. I could feel my spirits lifting. I wanted to touch his hand, but he seemed tense.

"After I get back I'll be a free man. I wanted you to know that, too." He smiled again. Before I could say anything he flung his jacket over his shoulder and left.

A week later Notch Callaway, the head of research, knocked on my office door and stuck his head in. "Congratulations," he said, a broad smile on his attractive, deeply lined face. "Looks like you'll have three years of NIMH funding. Your Biofeedback grant got a high score." He picked a paper clip from my desk and sat down. "You're going to be hiring people," he said, twisting the clip with his fingers. "There'll be people here who need funding. Before you hire we should talk."

"Of course."

After he left, I felt giddy with the pleasure of having a grant and bringing in money. Grants and papers were the royal road to academic success. Now I was a serious player.

I was happy. I was excited. My house smelled like an Indian oven. Yet my panics kept coming.

I sat in my office getting over an attack when Leo Rothstein, Vice Chairman of Psychiatry, called and said, "I'd like you to give the Anxiety Lecture to the freshmen medical students."

It was an honor; each department gave only a few freshman lectures, and their best teachers were chosen. Ordinarily, I would've jumped at the chance, but now I wasn't sure what I could do.

"I, uh…"

"You can talk about some of your own work. It'll be terrific."

"But, I …"

"We want the students to see the successful women in our department. Women are over thirty percent of the class these days. They need role models. Seeing you will reassure them."

Watching me run off the stage screaming won't be all that reassuring.

"So, Dr. Raskin, are you on board, or not?"

"I'll be happy to give the lecture."

"But I can't do it," I told Ruesch, pacing frantically before him as he sat with his back to his desk. "Thinking of a hundred and twenty students staring up at me makes me want to puke."

"Then weasel out. Get sick at the last minute. But don't agree to lecture again. Learn to say things like —I don't do well in front of large groups, but I'm good in small ones. Maybe I could teach medical students on their clerkships." He sat forward with his thick fingers pressed together. "Remember, you don't have to jump through every hoop."

I wasn't ready to weasel out and look bad in this hospital where I was finally getting ahead. I had lunch with Richard and we agreed that to get through my lecture I should go on Tofranil, an anti-depressant that stops panics, but can have difficult-to- tolerate side effects — dry mouth, constipation, weight gain, mental changes. Richard wrote me a prescription, and that evening I took the first dose, a very small one and felt cut off from myself. Richard wanted me to try another antidepressant. I wasn't sure what to do but decided to do nothing until the lecture time was closer. Usually putting off a worry was impossible for me, but I had an unusual distraction. Deva was back.

Chapter 15. Deva

We went to an Indian restaurant in San Francisco where we laughed and smiled and picked at our food. For me, this dinner was about sitting across from this man, having him lean toward me, touch my hand, without my heart flying out of my body. And I did start feeling comfortable, until we went back to my house where we sat in two club chairs, watching Arco roll on his back. Sex was coming although we didn't know when. We were close, yet distant; we knew each other, yet we didn't. The tension pressed down on the room, making it hard to lift iced tea to our lips or make comments. We sat like that for almost an hour. At the door, Deva took a deep breath and kissed me lightly on the lips. He looked happy, and banged his fists against his chest, Tarzan fashion.

Deva came by that week to meet the children. He asked what they liked to do. Keith took Deva to his room where Deva sat on the floor looking at Keith's drawings and making comments. Ali showed him her collection of knee socks, along with the scarves that matched them. Deva asked her to model a few. She did it with pleasure.

Deva started sleeping over when the children were with Michael. Then he spent a weekend with the three of us.

Saturday morning, I arrived in the kitchen to find him already there. I made coffee while he sat cross-legged on a chair munching a bowl of Special K. Ali showed up in her blue terry robe, yawning.

Deva said hello. Ali nodded, sauntered to the table, looked in Deva's bowl, and asked for Special K too. Keith, already dressed, came down a few minutes later. Half-way through his usual bacon and eggs, he said he had an important meeting of his Save-the-Animals club that afternoon. Then Deva announced he wanted to make us an authentic Indian dinner.

Ali and I took Arco to Julius Kahn Park for his afternoon run. When we got home, I felt a jolt of pleasure seeing Deva's banged-up yellow Plymouth in front of the house. Deva, looking like some four-armed Hindu god, was rushing around the kitchen turning chicken breasts in the broiler, testing potatoes, shaking *pakoras* in a skillet, and turning *roti* on a grill.

"Can I help?"

"Everything's under control," he said, smiling and rushing about.

After we finished eating, Deva sat taller, a formal expression on his face. "So Ali," he asked, "How did your day go?"

Ali looked surprised. She thought, then talked about taking Arco to the park, and how he played with Charlie, the poodle, and Cowgirl, a spotted mutt. When Deva turned to Keith to ask his question, Keith was ready. He said the president of his club had told one of the members, in confidence, that he flushed his sick goldfish down the toilet. That boy told everyone else.

"So what happened?" Deva asked.

"We suspended them both, but the boy who told the secret was suspended for longer."

After some discussion, Deva said it sounded like a fair decision.

The kids went off to play, leaving Deva with me at the table. "You're good with them," I said.

"Well, I'm the oldest of nine. I had a hand in raising my younger brothers and sisters. Besides I like these kiddoes." And he did like them; he liked them even before he met them. He seemed to want a ready-made family. I felt lucky. Many of my friends were meeting men who got upset when there were any children around, including their own.

Later, we made a fire in the den, something I'd rarely done since Michael left. We all got pillows and stretched in front of crackling flames.

"My dad would like your mom," Deva told the kids as he moved small logs with the brass poker. "He'd like that she's a doctor in a hospital, not out to make a lot of money. He's a doctor too, Ayurvedic. He's eighty now, but he still sees patients, still grinds his own prescriptions. Patients line up in our courtyard early in the morning, and he sees whoever's there. The patients pay what they can. Often nothing."

"Nothing," Keith repeated.

"Oh, maybe a chicken after several visits. That's a good payment. My dad's an incredible man. He went to jail for Gandhi. That makes him a hero in our village, but he doesn't care. He just does his work."

Deva was looking into the fire smiling to himself. I missed New York, but I couldn't imagine what it would be like to leave a family, a continent, a culture.

Deva not only liked the children around; he liked a full house. We took to having people over for dinner. Deva, a relaxed comfortable host, was interested in everyone. He'd sit down with each guest, and listen intently.

When we didn't have plans in the city, we'd often go to Berkeley to see a tall, talkative woman named Lois, and her quiet husband, Hal. They were Deva's oldest friends in the states. He met Lois at a community college where he was taking literature to polish his English, and she was taking it out of boredom. Lois had Deva to dinner, she helped with his English, and she introduced him to her best friend — Susan. Eager to recreate a tight foursome, Lois was exceptionally nice to me. Deva said she'd moved all her pictures of Susan out of view.

On a late November afternoon, I was watering the Bayberry in front of the house when I saw a gray pickup truck with Deva in the back, his white shirt billowing out behind him as he worked to hold down a mattress, boxes, a floor lamp, chairs, and bookcases. We'd been together about a month and hadn't talked about his moving in, but the truck pulled up in front of my house. The driver was a woman with short blond hair.

"Susan this is Marjorie," Deva said, jumping out. "Marjorie, Susan."

Susan's face was puffy from crying. She nodded hello. I nodded back and quickly went inside. I watched them from behind a curtained window. Susan sat quietly as Deva moved his things into the garage. Then he stood beside the truck, and they talked for a long time. Before she drove off, he tousled her hair. I'd look out every so often and see him sitting on the front stairs with his back to the house. What was he feeling? What was I feeling? I wasn't sure. I was pleased that he still cared so much about someone he was leaving, but I was jealous too. And I wondered if I'd end up crying like her. I wished I knew why they'd broken up.

Deva came in smiling, but looked tense. He said he wanted some things around for when he slept over, and he'd store the rest in my garage until he found an apartment. I knew there wouldn't be an apartment. He was moving in. It wasn't wise, and I didn't like his being devious about it, but I didn't protest. I wanted him with me. I was happy when he was in the house. I laughed a lot. I was less anxious.

But my relative calm was disrupted two weeks later when Dr. Rothstein's secretary called, asking if I was using slides in my lecture. It was in a month. After that, I was in an almost constant panic. Richard thought I should try another medication, but I was afraid. Deva rubbed my head, my hands, my feet, and tried to find the pressure points that would calm me. He even put my feet in icy water, because, he said, that might drain blood from the brain. That month he put the kids to bed; he cooked our dinners.

On the day of the lecture I wore a red dress with white piping, trying to cheer myself up. I didn't have any breakfast and kept coughing from nerves. Deva drove me to work. Somehow I got through the morning and, in the afternoon found myself up on stage clutching the microphone with wet fingers and shouting into a sea of bright white jackets. My voice sounded odd, but I kept going. I saw vague images of myself, running, screaming, falling to the floor. These things felt about to happen. To ignore them, I shouted louder and louder. The fluorescent lights flickered above me, the white jackets glared in my eyes, my heart beat so fast, my chest hurt. I held the podium with all my strength. I heard applause, and I was off the stage, blinking, rubbing my chest and listening to questions.

Faces came into focus. A female medical student with large eyes and pale moist skin asked if we could talk in private. Another student, a male, said he wanted to call me. A circle of students stood asking detailed questions about anxiety and panic. I relaxed as I talked with them. Back then anxiety was a mysterious subject, and I felt good about reaching some people who'd probably been worrying in silence.

On the drive home, I told Deva I could never go through that again, even if it cost me my job. Deva said I wouldn't lose my job. After all I was teaching, doing research, and publishing papers. "Relax," he said. "The ordeal's over." And I did relax for almost a year.

Chapter 16. The Almosts

Michael came by one Saturday morning, saying he wanted to talk in private. "I think I've found her," he said, standing in the living room facing the back windows. I sat in a chair before him.

I tried to smile. "That's great. So what's she like, your special lady?"

"She's English. Well, really, Regina's lived all over. She's fantastic — honest, warm, gorgeous. I've known her a couple of months, but unless there's some hidden secret, she's the one."

I'd heard that people in love glowed, but that morning I saw it.

"You'll like her, she's interested in psychology. It's what she'll do next. She used to model, but she likes to help people. Oh, she's a bit younger than we are, but she's no kid."

"Have the children met her yet? They haven't said anything."

"They've met her a few times."

"And they like her?"

"Of course. She's young and energetic. She has all these great stories. Ali thinks she's beautiful."

A pang of jealousy struck me.

Michael went on about Regina's virtues until the kids bounded in with Arco. Ali ran across the room in her orange and yellow knee socks, kissed me on the cheek, hugged her father, then plopped on the floor beside Keith. He was kneeling down trying to photograph Arco with his paws in the air. I watched the children, feeling that I was

111

seeing them at a distance. Ali was almost six, Keith almost eleven. They were healthy, happy kids. They liked school, had friends, and were back to laughing a lot. Ali was the volatile outspoken one, Keith her quiet protector. I felt proud of them and proud that Michael and I had done right by them. I told myself not to think about Regina. My concern was with the children.

I knew that when Michael met someone I'd feel bad, but I didn't expect to feel so flattened. Deva was working at the hospital and I thought of driving up to see him, but pictured myself crashing into a concrete wall. Then I imagined Michael at the scene, a woman in a long white satin gown on his arm. "Yes, that's Marge," he'd say. "Never was too stable." A burst of anger shot through me. I got up and put a stack of records on the phonograph to distract myself.

Later, I called Deva.

"Michael's in love," I said. "Her name's Regina. She's a young, beautiful English woman who's lived all over. And get this — she's a former model and psychologist-to-be."

"Boy. Not, what I expected from old Michael. And how're you doing?"

"I've been better."

"I'll finish up here and come home. Bet you twenty she's a nut."

Deva and I had been together for almost a year, and the sense of fullness in the house was even stronger. Even better, we weren't turning into a brother sister act. But Deva had ways that made me uneasy. He and Susan spoke every week, and if she had problems he'd pop over. I still didn't understand why they broke up. He would say lots of different things about it, but his words made nothing clearer. Also, much of his past was cloaked in mystery. When he was a teenager he'd run away from home and lived on his own in New Delhi, but I couldn't tell if that was a matter of days or years, or how he lived. I often pushed him to untangle the past, but the more he spoke about it, the foggier it grew.

I relaxed when I heard Deva's car pull up in the driveway. He ambled though the house, tossed his jacket on the sofa, sat on the arm of my chair, and rubbed my neck. I leaned against him, and we stayed like that for a while.

"I feel bad," I said, knowing I'd regret my words. "Michael's going to remarry, and we're in this limbo."

Deva took my hand. "I love you, girl. As far as I'm concerned, we are married. It's only a piece of paper."

"No, it's much more than that."

"Well, maybe someday. But it's complicated. Look, why would you want more — I'm here with you most of the time."

"I guess."

"I'm always here when you need me. Right?"

"Mostly."

He smiled, but I didn't smile back. He liked living in an eternal present, but I wanted an agreed-upon future. I often talked about it with Frieda. She backed me, saying things weren't working out with Deva. But I didn't want to hear that either.

"Why don't you all come over tomorrow," Michael said on the phone that evening. "Come and meet Regina." I felt a churning in my belly. I'd just heard about the woman, now I had to meet her. I slept poorly and in the morning my face was puffy. After making oatmeal for the kids, I lay on my bed with a green mud-pack drying on my face and wet tea bags over my eyes. Ali came in, peeked under the tea bags, and stayed to supervise my dressing. I ended up wearing beige slacks and a V-necked aqua sweater. I thought I looked matronly, but she was pleased.

It was late afternoon when Deva, the kids, and I walked up three flights of stairs to Michael's apartment. He was standing in the doorway, holding a tall drink topped with a slice of lime. As Michael made introductions, Regina rose from the couch. He hadn't exaggerated: she was gorgeous — high cheekbones, greenish brown eyes, shining red hair, and a lean, sexy body.

"I am so happy to meet you," Regina said, holding out a lightly freckled arm. "Michael always says the nicest things about you."

"He says wonderful things about you too," I answered, shaking Regina's hand.

"We're having Gin and Tonic's," Michael said. "Sound okay?"

We nodded and sat across the marble coffee table facing Regina. On it was a basket of crackers, a platter with wedges of Camembert and Cheddar cheese, and a bowl of Bosc pears. While Michael fixed the drinks, Regina smiled at me with an expectant expression. I tried to think of something to say, but nothing came to mind.

After our second drink, talking was easier. Deva went on about wanting to bring his family to the states. Regina spoke about becoming a psychologist. At least here I found things to say to her. Michael sat back proudly, a drink in his hand. I wondered what possessed him to want to be with someone psychologically minded again.

The kids were staying with Michael and Regina for dinner. On the way out, Ali whispered, "You were good, Mom." She was smiling, and at first I felt bad, thinking she'd been worried about me. But her pleased smile made me realize that she didn't want me to be more beautiful or funnier than Regina. She just wanted a solid, presentable mom.

Deva and I drove to Oakland to do some shopping, and I started in again on our being in limbo.

"Whatever I say, I can't win," Deva complained.

We did some shopping, and I was touchy. "Difficult" Deva called it.

I was "difficult" for the next several days. One evening after we'd been quarreling, Deva said that maybe it was time for another of his mountain hikes. He'd gone on mountain hikes twice since I'd been with him, and each time he'd come back looking restored. I agreed; I didn't want to say things I'd regret later. I had a grant report to send in. Deva said he'd go after helping with the statistics.

I'd done a follow up on my pilot subjects six months after their biofeedback training, and although a third improved, their improvement was not related to learning to relax. At our research meeting we were trying to understand why those subjects got better. Most improved was the Jamaican nurse whose mother had left her alone for days. Steve, one of the trainers, a sweet young man with a bushy mustache, said the nurse had befriended the research group. When she had problems at work, or good news, she'd come by or call. On her birthday, she brought us cake. As we went through the list of improved subjects, all had formed a similar, but less intense, relationship with us. It could have all been a placebo response, but these findings fit with my view of severe anxiety. Many abused or neglected children crave attachment as an adult, but mistrust people too much to let them close. Sometimes distant relationships like the one to our research group provide a partial solution. Intense relationships you can't fully count on can help too, although I wasn't thinking much about that then.

After we'd completed our report, Deva planned his trip — a ten day hike at Zion National Park. After leaving, he called me several times from pay phones to announce where he was. In fact he called so often, I grew suspicious. His last call was at eleven in the evening, and as soon as he hung up, I called Susan. She didn't answer. And she didn't answer at one, two, three, or five. I lay in bed feeling sick. Early in the morning I called Susan's friend Lois, to ask if Susan was with Deva. Lois hemmed and hawed. I asked again, and when she said I was putting her in an awkward position, I went to the bathroom and threw up.

Deva called that evening. "How are you?" he asked, his voice wildly cheerful.

"How do think I am when you're off with Susan."

"Me with Susan? Where did you ever…"

"You're disgusting." I hung up.

I called Frieda for the third time that day to tell her about Deva. She listened, expressing nothing but surprise. When I ran out of words, she asked if I had the kids that weekend. I didn't. "Why don't we get out of town?" she asked. "It'd be nice to get away. We could drive up to the Russian River and stay over on Saturday night." I readily agreed. I didn't want to be alone with my feelings.

Late the next night, Deva arrived at my door, his clothes rumpled, his face unshaven. We went in the bedroom to talk.

"I was alone," he said. "How can I convince you?"

"You weren't alone. I called Susan. She's away too."

"Well, when she gets back you'll talk to her. She'll tell you where she was."

"That's crazy. Of course she'll lie."

Deva unbuttoned his shirt to change, and it made me nervous to see his body. He had a long tan chest with a few tufts of curly black hair around his nipples. He stood with his shirt open, saying over and over that he was alone and that he loved me. I saw his white teeth, his white shirt hanging at the sides of his chest, his white sneakers. I wanted to pull him to me and believe everything he said.

He started to come closer, and I said, "Just take what you need and go. We'll worry about you getting the rest of your things later."

I went down to kitchen, turned on the floodlight, and looked out at the garden. The leaves of the plum tree looked silver in the evening light. I'm not sure how long I sat there, or if I answered when Deva called to me. When I heard his car drive away, I felt like crying, but didn't. I told myself this is right. You don't need him.

Over the next days, I felt like the world's most virtuous person. I cleaned the house, weeded the yard, picked broken glass off the street, and did all the paper work that had sat on my desk for months. I sent pictures of the children to my parents and my aunt Beaty. I wasn't demeaning myself in that awful relationship. I couldn't get calls that would make me sick. In the evenings Amanda came over with Billy and we made hamburgers and Tater Tots, or spaghetti with meatballs. I put my Indian spices in the back of the closet. I had a small silver friendship ring Deva's sister had sent me. It was pretty and looked like a wedding band. I put it in a drawer under my gloves.

As we drove up to Russian River, Frieda told me where things stood with Ray. She'd be able to leave for New York, but they kept fighting about everything else. When we turned off at the River, the sun was bright, and young women in shorts were selling food off the back of a truck. We got juice from them, and they showed us the road to our motel. We spent most of the afternoon swimming in a dammed-up section of the Russian River. It was cold, but if I moved quickly, I didn't feel it. As I swam, doing backstrokes, I pushed away my sadness.

That night, there were only a few customers in the diner. It was damp and poorly lit with a broken jukebox in front, and the few customers looked lonely. Occasional tears slipped down my cheeks, but I wiped them away and talked about the scenery and the river. Frieda understood, and kept the conversation going. But when we got back to our cabin, I burst out crying. I couldn't stand not holding Deva again. Not seeing his grin. Not walking beside him. Frieda listened as I went on and on.

"You know," she said. "Deva's an almost. They're the ones that really kill you."

That helped. Later, after she was sleeping I thought more about her words. If Deva was an almost, maybe there'd be a someone — someone to love without all this pain. I thought then that my main problem was a lack of reasonable men. I hadn't forgotten Phillip, or that I'd panicked when he'd gotten too close, but that was tucked away in another part of my mind.

At home I was lonely, and on the verge of panic. Ali made cookies so I'd feel better. I did strenuous yoga that calmed me for a couple of hours. At the hospital, Deva kept looking at me like he was ready to come back.

Deva and I met for coffee. We met for dinner. We had dinner again, and he stayed over. I brought the Indian spices to the front of the closet. I put the silver ring back on. All right, I wasn't so high on virtue, but I was happy, or almost happy. He loved me. I loved him. Why should I ask for more?

Things were both the same and different. I knew what I had with this man. Not only had he run off with Susan, but he did it so I'd find out. I thought of him as a wild horse who'd meet me each day in the pasture, unless I tried to saddle him. Could I stay with him knowing what he was like? I told myself I could, but settling for far less than I needed kept me angry. I felt contempt for him because he couldn't stay with anyone, and contempt for myself for staying with him. This came out in snide remarks. Deva got his own apartment, but mostly he lived with me. We got lonely when we were apart. I got anxious. And we still had our good days.

Some months later, in the spring of 1976, Frieda left for New York. Before she went Deva and I threw a big party for her at my house. She came in a blue silk outfit: a beaded silk top with narrow straps and full-bottomed trousers. She looked beautiful with slender gold earrings swinging against her neck and her dark eyes shinning. Deva was at his best making *Pakoras,* passing them around, and talking with everyone. When Frieda cried, he put his arm around her and said we'd visit her soon. After I put the kids to bed, the mood in the room changed. It became sad and sexy with almost everyone smoking pot. I didn't smoke because getting stuck in the middle of a sentence frightened me. Frieda began to dance, leaps and twirls and graceful one-legged stances. Then she moved her hips like a belly dancer, bending back until her head almost touched the floor behind her. She came up slowly, hips swaying from side to side. We formed a chain around her and danced too. As loneliness threatened the room, we whirled faster and faster.

Chapter 17. Philip

That summer I went to hear some papers being read at a big Psychiatric meeting in San Francisco. I wore my black dress, and had my hair pulled back. I felt plain and pleased with myself for not caring.

When the first lecture was over, I waited in the hall.

"I'm so glad to see you," said a familiar voice. I couldn't move. There was Philip. "I'm sorry I was so nasty at the end," he said. "You did what you had to."

I nodded. Philip looked like himself with his blue-green eyes and broad shoulders.

"You got me through Medical school. I know that now. Worked it all out in my analysis. I wanted to thank you in person. Never thought it would take this long."

I smiled, but felt tearful. Philip was married now, with four kids. I'd followed his life through friends. I knew his mother died a couple of years after we broke up. I'd wanted to call him, but felt it wouldn't be welcome. I heard that after she died, he got a bleeding ulcer, and the bleeding went on for weeks.

"I wanted to call you," I said. "I wanted to say I was sorry about your mom. And then I was worried about you."

"I expected her to go, you know that. But when it happened, I couldn't take it. My analysis stopped my bleeding. Really, my analyst came to the hospital every day. But I don't want to go into that now. How are you?"

He moved closer. I wanted to touch him at the side of his face where his sideburns were shaved and the bristles looked so red.

"Hey, my kid brother's getting married. Isn't that something. But you — two kids, that's terrific. How are you?"

Those green blue eyes were fixed on me. I wished I'd fixed myself up that morning.

"I'm fine. Just fine."

"No, tell me the truth." There was a line between his eyebrows.

I laughed. "The real truth. The whole truth."

"Yes."

"Okay. Not one bit changed. Two tries at analysis, and not one bit changed. I still can't get together with someone I love."

"Hey, don't give up on yourself. I know you can be all right. I always said that. Remember?"

Say you love me. I know you're faithful.

We stood looking at each. Philip said, "I read your papers. I liked them."

"I know your work. Wow, director of training at Mass General. That's terrific."

"It's Okay. Lots of politics. Too much politics." He smiled.

God he was something. He was the best. I'd let go of the best.

People were going in to the next lecture. Philip gestured me ahead, his right hand close to my waist, but not touching. My cheeks were hot, and my hands trembled. "You know, I better get back to work." I quickly shook his hand. "So. Great seeing you."

I rushed out of the building and down the stone steps. The sunshine blinded me for a moment, but I kept going. I wanted to cry. I wanted to run back and hug him.

Chapter 18. Freezing in San Francisco

I spent a lot of time going back and forth in my mind, trying to decide if I should return to New York. I was thinking about it on a Monday evening in November, when Sarah called, asking me to drive up to U.C. Hospital to read Richard's chart. He'd had a thyroid biopsy that afternoon, been told there was nothing to worry about, but left surgery convinced he was dying.

He was in a private room with a plastic table at the side. He sat up when he saw me, scratching at the bandages on his neck. "Sperling, my surgeon, started out full of jokes. Then his face changed. It was awful. He couldn't look me in the eye. Didn't even come by later. He's a fucking coward, but I got the message."

"We don't know anything for sure," Sarah said firmly. "Maybe Sperling's wife told him he had to be on time for dinner. Maybe he forgot you. It happens."

"Oh, Sarah … please." Richard turned away. Sarah sat on the bed. I went to the nurse's station.

The charge nurse, Annie Plaut, a stout blond, had a brusque efficiency I'd come to respect. She glanced at my I.D. tag, then handed me the chart. I flipped through to the operating note, expecting some description of the nodule, a statement about the frozen section, a guess even. "There's almost nothing here," I said to Mrs. Plaut.

"I know. Sometimes those surgeons get careless."

I reached for the large black phone and dialed Sperling's service. Sperling couldn't be reached, and the doctor covering for him knew nothing about Richard's case. I put the phone back in its cradle, but held on to it, wondering whom to call next. Helen Redkin, the person who was often my lab partner in Medical School, was doing a pathology fellowship at U.C. I beeped her. Yes, given time, she could find the frozen section report.

Richard was deep in a drugged contentment. Sarah sat off to the side, next to the table, her eyes closed and her lips moving. She finished what I thought was a prayer and looked at me with frightened eyes. I told her the chart said little, that probably Sperling was rushing. I told her about Helen, too.

"Thanks," she said, hoisting a big floral tote onto her lap.

"Would you like a tangerine? Some grapes?" Sarah put a paper-plate on the table and covered it with bunches of concord grapes. "They're really nice ones," she said. "Sweet and juicy." She asked after Keith and Alexis, but I didn't have too much to report. She said Rachel was getting into everything; last night she tried to play in the Kitty Litter. Sarah laughed when I described Keith at two, tearing through a restaurant, grabbing ice out of people's glasses. I found myself relaxing, as if we were in Sarah's kitchen, then glumly remembered where we were.

Mrs. Plaut called me to the phone.

"A Lymphoma," Helen said. "And not a good one. Of course you can't be sure until the whole path report's in. Let me know what happens."

I turned to Mrs. Plaut, but her chair was empty. The florescent lights gave off a bluish cast that made everything around me look flat. I'd tell them Lymphoma, but that was all I'd say. By the time I left, Richard was sitting up in bed, thinking of doctors to call while Sarah took notes. Both of them were repeating "at least it has a cure." Remembering Helen's words, I wanted to yell out don't be so damn hopeful.

I drove home slowly. Deva had left the outside lights on, and as I got closer I saw lights in the upstairs and downstairs halls. I went up to where the children were sleeping. Ali was in the bottom bunk, her honey colored hair splayed out against the pillow. I tucked her white comforter with its tiny yellow roses around her, and kissed her tanned cheek. In her sleep she wiped off my kiss. I watched her for a while, then went up the ladder to check on Keith who was sleeping with his head flung back and his mouth open. His hair had a slightly sour smell. I stroked it. I stood by the bunkbeds, thinking that if I watched these children closely I could protect them from anything. It was the kind of thinking I had as a kid.

In the spill of hall light I saw Deva in the bedroom asleep on top of the covers, wearing jeans and a T-shirt. He woke up as soon as I came in, and asked what happened.

"Awful, awful," he repeated. When I got to Helen's comments, he sprang out of bed, saying we needed wine.

I changed into a nightgown and stretched my legs out under the covers. Deva brought up a bottle of white wine, and two juice glasses. The wine had a hint of vinegar. That felt right; I didn't want to drink anything that tasted too good.

"Jesus," Deva said, shaking his head. "It's so crazy. Forty with a young wife and daughter."

"That'll help get him through."

"If he comes through."

"Don't say that. I don't even want to think it."

"I always wanted to be a doctor." Deva said quietly. "I started Med school in India. I got this young girl as a patient, about fifteen, smart, big eyes, glasses, a sweet smile. She had pneumonia. I'd examine her every day and say not to worry — we can cure pneumonia. She was dead in two weeks. After that I quit."

I felt closer to Deva. At times I was seeing him as a life partner again.

The U.C. doctors wanted Richard to get his treatment at Stanford. It's a center for Hodgkins and Lymphoma. Richard was pleased because Linden, the doctor he was to see, was considered humane as well as brilliant. When I called Richard to find out how his first appointment went, he sounded upset. He said he couldn't understand what Linden was saying. I asked if I could help. "Yes," he said. "Our next appointment's Friday. I'd like you to come. Maybe you can understand him. Maybe we just get too nervous."

It was cold the morning Sarah picked me up. She wore a maroon wool coat and a black scarf with a border of large red roses. Richard was dressed up as well. Gray tweed coat. Gray hat. Polished black leather shoes.

We sat in a large waiting room holding magazines on our laps. Every time someone's name was called we looked over the top of our magazines. If the person looked very sick, Richard and Sarah looked down quickly. After a while my stomach hurt, so I went to the gift shop to buy Tums. I'd just come back when Richard's name was called.

We went down a long corridor to a small room with an examining table. Linden was a tall friendly man, with glasses that slipped down his nose. There was a button missing on his shirt from which black hairs protruded. My first thought was why doesn't someone clean him up. He talked mostly about chemical reactions. I didn't understand him either. The three of us exchanged glances; then Sarah and I started pushing him to say things simply. This took work on his part and ours. After a while it grew clear: he wanted Richard to choose between a standard treatment with a fair remission rate, and a new, aggressive, but dangerous regime that could cure.

Richard was still seated on the examining table, rubbing his hand over his mouth. He looked at Linden. "What do you suggest?"

Linden eyes swept over Richard several times, then he looked at Sarah. He took a deep breath and blew it out. "If I were you, I'd go for the cure."

Richard jumped from the table and kissed him.

We were hungry, but we wanted to get far away from Stanford to eat. Sarah drove back to San Francisco and we went to a Kosher restaurant she'd heard about from friends. It said health food, but was really a Deli with pastrami, corned beef, and chopped liver. After lunch, Richard tipped his hat back on his head, and started laughing from deep in his belly. "Pastrami for white cells, chopped liver for red ones, pickles for platelets, maybe." Sarah laughed too, tears flowing from her eyes. Then I joined in. We were like kids: every time our eyes met we howled. The waiters shrugged their shoulders, mouthed "drugs."

My divorce was final, and in it was a provision for me to live anywhere in the United States with the children. Michael agreed, in part because of our initial five-year agreement about moving back to New York. But I think the bigger reason was that Regina's father was ill and he felt pressure to marry quickly. A big wedding was being planned in London.

After Richard started chemo, his house became a drop-in center. Young men from his shul came, rabbis, and people who'd just been diagnosed with their own cancers. Richard sat in the living room, usually with his tweed coat on, trying to give advice to the cancer patients. He'd made a point of getting to know about the oncologists in the Bay area, and about cancer drugs, alternative treatments, and insurance issues. Sarah, her hair shiny and her dresses brightly colored, was forever bringing snacks to the table. Rachel would toddle through in patterned pajamas. She'd curl up on Richard's lap, and he'd kiss her belly until she giggled. I was amazed, but Richard was happy.

When I was alone with him, he'd ask how my life was going. I'd tell him I was fine. I had no news.

One afternoon we were sitting behind Richard's house under an oak tree. He'd asked how I was and I gave my usual answers.

"That's hard to believe," he said. "You were always breaking off with Deva, every other week. That just stopped?"

"How can I talk about boyfriend trouble when you're fighting cancer?"

"How can you not? I'm not an invalid cut off from the world."

I spent my life hiding my problems, and now I was asked to share them. I didn't instantly come gushing out with my worries, but slowly I got used to conversations in which I talked about my confusion over Deva, while Richard told me about fluctuations in his white count. I told him my thoughts about going back to New York; he spoke about his worries over Sarah and Rachel. We didn't have answers for each other, but we listened.

I found myself trying to extract forever-after type of promises from Deva, and got flip answers. I didn't tell Richard about those interchanges, but I did tell him I planned to look for work in New York. He was pleased and optimistic about something turning up. We drank carrot juice to our futures.

The children and I had story time before they went to bed. We had two main characters: Fateo the detective and Half-Penny Gertie, girl sleuth.

I'd start the story: "Fateo was called to find a woman's missing brother. The brother was rich and he lived in the Marina. Fateo went to his house."

"Bad men pushed Fateo into the water," said Ali. "Alligators came after him."

"There are no alligators in the Marina," Keith corrected. "Men came in a submarine with ray guns."

"And Alligators."

"Fateo hid behind a rock," I went on. "He saw the submarine, and lots of briefcases filled with gold. The submarine went past him, with a thug driving."

Somehow I did my job: I kept Fateo safe and had him solve his case. I enjoyed story time. The kids were imaginative and funny, and made me laugh until I cried. I remembered that sometimes I could make my parents laugh like that too.

After Richard's chemo stopped, he put on weight, and his hair and beard grew back. He talked about forming a clinic for cancer patients. Sarah was to get training and be part of it. Stephan, a friend from the Berkeley School of Health, was helping them get a grant. Richard organized a trip to Mexico and smuggled in Laetrile. He was busy, and I didn't see him for several weeks, although we often talked on Friday evenings.

In October of 1977 I stayed with Frieda in Manhattan and interviewed for jobs. There was more work available than I'd expected. I had some tentative offers and was supposed to make a final decision by Christmas. But when I returned to San Francisco, I was afraid to make the move. It was such a big step, and I couldn't face uprooting the kids. For them it might be worse than the divorce. I was determined to make San Francisco work for me. I saw a lot of Amanda, while trying to make new friends. And I made a couple of good ones: Nancy, a widow and writer, and Shirley, a divorcee who did research. I saw Deva often, but made efforts to meet new men as well. I joined hiking clubs, went to weekend seminars, and had blind dates. But the finding-men part was discouraging.

One early spring afternoon while I was working in a medication clinic, the secretary said a couple were waiting to see me, but had no appointment. I looked out front and saw Richard and Sarah, sitting on the benches like an old couple. I knew this was bad news and didn't want to see them.

They walked behind me into my office and sat quietly. Richard was gaunt, and Sarah had dark rings under her eyes. They were dressed up, and Richard held a large flat package.

"It's in my bone marrow," he said, after sitting down. "Linden is going to keep trying things, but well, we're at a new level now. I got this book about lymphoma written by the Stanford group. I want you to keep it. I can't read this stuff anymore."

I took the book. I know we spoke, but I don't remember what we said. I know we hugged a lot. After they left I sat for a long time not believing what was happening. Then I thought about time. How it had limits. How I had to decide what I wanted. Was I staying with Deva? Was I going back to New York? Hanging above my desk was a 1978 calendar with a different Van Gogh print for each month. Starry Night was there for April. I kept looking at it. My grandmother Ethel, my father's mother, had framed Van Gogh prints in her apartment in Williamsburg, and Van Goghs always reminded me of her. I missed my parents. I missed Beaty. I missed Mollie and Mike and my three cousins.

Deva had dinner on the table. I told him about the new complication. He held me. Later I called Frieda to tell her.

Richard's house was no longer a drop-in center. His own rabbi came regularly, so did a few of the young men, and many of the new cancer patients. The rage that must've been gathering in Richard all this time boiled over. One of the rabbis who had stopped coming was a silver-tongued man who spoke of love. Richard called to tell him he was a hypocrite. Then he had a big fight with Linden and wanted another doctor. It took weeks to patch that up.

Over the next months Richard was in and out of hospitals. In an hour Sarah would transform a hospital room into a familiar space. She came armed with posters, rugs, blankets, pillows, pictures of Rachel, and all kinds of food. I'd watch her just keep going. When Richard talked about her need to remarry, she covered her ears.

Deva was always around ready to take the kids. So was Amanda. So were Michael and Regina.

During the spring one hospitalization kept stretching out. Richard said he was in pain, but holding out against taking Morphine until Sarah was ready. Morphine would constipate him and lead to an overwhelming infection. Sarah spent a lot of time praying, then she said she was ready. She called me at home one evening, and told me to come to the hospital to say goodbye to Richard. I hesitated. I didn't like saying good-byes.

"You have to come," Sarah said. "Not for Richard, but for you."

I was startled that Sarah could be so generous at a time like that. I got dressed and saw Richard once before he went into a coma. I held his hand and he smiled.

He died that night at four AM. It was November, 1978.

My next weeks were full. I went to sit *shiva* every night for a week. I spent time with Sarah. Her mother was with her, and her sister from Israel. A few months later Sarah and Rachel left for Israel to live with Sarah's sister. There wasn't enough money for her to keep the house in Berkeley and send Rachel to religious school. I was anxious and numb, but mostly I felt cold. I had the sense I'd freeze in San Francisco.

Chapter 19. Going Home Again

I sublet an apartment on West Ninth Street in a brick building with gray stone columns, carved wooden doors, and above the doors were small glass squares in red, blue, and yellow. The block had the look of old New York. I saw that most in the evenings when the air took on a reddish cast, and the rows of lanterns, now electric, glowed silver against the buildings. But it was 1979 and three thousand people lived on that one block.

The city bristled with possibilities. Walking to my new job at Beth Israel, I often crossed paths with a man with smiling green eyes who'd nod good morning. And in the hospital cafeteria I'd watch all the earnest doctors in rumpled white coats, thinking my future husband might sit across the table, maybe it would be just that easy. Beth Israel had a small friendly psych department where I supervised medical students rotating through. At different medical meetings in the city, old classmates welcomed me back. And Frieda gave a brunch for me soon after I arrived.

But the city that excited me overwhelmed my children. They were with me for July and August because Michael couldn't keep them in San Francisco that first summer. They were also furious at me for dragging them away from their father, their friends, and Deva who'd taken Arco. I tried to talk them into spending time at my parent's summer-house in the Adirondacks. When they refused I hired a young woman to watch them, but it was not a success.

One hot July day Ali drew a mural on the shower door and Keith started a fire in the skillet while trying to deep-fry an egg. When I came home that afternoon greasy black smoke was oozing from our windows. Keith and Ali sat nervously waiting. The woman caring for them announced she was quitting. I was overwhelmed with guilt and anger. I called my parents.

"Don't worry," my father said, sounding almost pleased. "I'll drive down first thing tomorrow. I'll get them to come back with me."

And my father was pleased. Not pleased that there was trouble, but pleased to feel like the head of the family again. He liked doing things for us, providing for us, using that logical mind of his to settle issues. When I was getting my divorce he'd said don't worry I won't let you fail. I'd counted on those words. I felt that as long as he was alive, I was safe and I mattered.

Armed with four hot-fudge Sundaes, he arrived early the next afternoon. For someone who'd just driven five hours he looked fresh with his muscular tan arms showing beneath a short sleeved white shirt. At seventy-four, he seemed at the height of his powers.

"Just spend one week in the country to see how you like it," my father said, licking the fudge from his spoon. "There are a lot of other children up there. We go swimming in a big lake, and there are canoes and rowboats. Grandma can't wait to see you. She's cooking for you right now."

The kids, who didn't have much choice, looked at each other and nodded. I promised to call them each evening and be up on Friday night. As we walked to my father's Oldsmobile, he kept up a steady stream of talk about all the things they'd do.

When I called during the week, Ali, all bubbly, told me she'd met two girls near her age. But Keith wanted to go back with me.

I drove out of the city Friday afternoon, had dinner in Albany, then continued on Route Nine toward Lake George. My parents lived in Fourth Lake, a community founded by a bunch of New York City school teachers back when the trip up took ten hours. It was still mainly a place for teachers who had the summer off.

Keith was pacing outside when I got to the house. I went inside to say hello, then joined him. We walked down a back road toward the Greger farm with its one horse, talking as we slapped back mosquitoes.

"I have nothing to do here," Keith said. "Ali goes off in the morning with her friends, but there are no kids my age. Grandma won't let me cross the highway so I can't go to the lake myself. I went down with her once and as soon as I was in the water she yelled for me to get out. Then, she tried to dry me off in front of everyone. It was awful."

I told Keith I'd take him back, but I wanted to talk with my mother first. I was sure we could work something out.

I went to my parents' room where my mother stood in front of her dresser, her hair in pink rollers. I sat on my mother's bed, watching her in the mirror as she rubbed Ponds Cold Cream into her cheeks. When I thanked her for all her help, she nodded. Then I talked about Keith — how it was hard on him because there were no kids his age, and how he wanted to go to the lake himself. She listened, still rubbing the cream in.

"He is thirteen," I said.

Her hands left her face and hovered over the dresser.

"Do you think, that maybe, you could change your highway rule?"

I saw the rage before she turned to me. "I'm doing you a favor. Either, accept the way I do things, or take them home. I'm too old to learn new tricks." She held her head high, but her hands were shaking.

I edged out of the room, feeling like I'd been pulled back into the worst of my own adolescence. It did occur to me briefly that suddenly being responsible for two children at her age, was overwhelming. But I told myself so what — one way or another she's always overwhelmed.

Keith came back with me, spent a boring week in the city, then stayed in the Adirondacks, reading, drawing and occasionally doing projects for my mother like putting up shelves. I drove up every Friday and stayed the weekend. I watched Mom and Dad with my children, feeling like I was spying on my own past. Dad took them on a three mile hike most afternoons to a local shop that made good, thin-crust pizza. When Mom didn't see them, she worried that they were about to drown, get run over, or catch pneumonia. I expected that, but her reaction to small problems made me feel like screaming. Ali wet her bed once and my mother wanted to push her face into the soiled sheets.

"You've got to stop this quickly, or no one will have her over," she said, the sheets under her arms, her eyes bulging.

When my mother talked like that, she repulsed me. She had a habit of spitting on her finger to take something off my face while I stood frozen. I hated to have her touch me.

When we got back to the city, Ali's mood fell. "I miss my Daddy," she kept saying.

I'd tell her to call him, but it didn't help. If she didn't reach him she'd be sad, and if she did, her longings grew worse.

"C'mon," Keith would say, "let's go out. We'll go the stores on Eighth Street. You like that."

Going out with Keith did help, and I expected school, which had just started, to help even more. They went to the Village Community School on West Tenth Street; a small progressive private school where fitting into classes that had been together for years was a problem. Ali entered in third grade, and Keith started eighth, but his situation was easier. He was up against a bully the class disliked, and since he was tall, strong and ready to fight, his problem calmed down after a couple of confrontations. In fact, he developed his own small following. Ali's class had popular kids, a central group, and out casts. Ali soon made friends with Beth, one of the outcasts. The class leaders immediately threw a party including Ali but not Beth. Ali didn't go and became an outsider too.

The kids couldn't wait for their Christmas vacation in San Francisco, but by Easter things had changed. When I picked them up at Newark Airport, they came down the ramp smiling, white nametags pinned to their clothes. Ali grinned when she saw me. They had friends in New York by then, and were beginning to explore Manhattan. Keith knew every shop on the Lower East Side that sold old comics. Ali was taking acting classes at the Herbert Berghof Studio on Sundays. One morning I met her after her class, and on the way home we passed Sazarac House, an old Cajun American restaurant on the corner of Hudson and Charles. Ali stopped in front of their brunch sign. "Maybe I'll be famous some day," she said. "Then we'd have brunch out a lot. Maybe we should practice." I took her in, and after being seated on the screened in porch, Ali slid her dark glasses back on her head, picked up a menu, and, her legs not quite reaching the floor, said, "Well, daahling, let's see what they have today?"

But it took years, maybe longer, for the strain of leaving their father to subside. Ali wrote school papers on being pulled away from her home, and Keith, considering himself the man of the house, grew ever more serious.

Before I knew it, it was summer again — the summer of 1980 — and the children were off to San Francisco to be with Michael. I'd never lived alone for two months before and getting through the summer felt like dragging myself through a desert. I tried to make plans for every weekend, but sometimes they fell through, and I ended up spending too much time alone. I began blaming myself whenever I felt lonely. I'd tell myself there must be a reason you're alone. You're too sad, too desperate, too pathetically needy, and people see it. Sometimes when I was in that mood, I'd look in the mirror, see my mother's eyes staring back at me, and want to crush my own head with a rock. I'd get a hand mirror, and standing by my dresser, study my face from every angle. I'd see myself as ugly, feel ashamed of what I was doing, yet I couldn't stop. The only way I found to break out of it was to talk to someone who cared about me. I'd call Frieda, or Amanda or Deva. And once when I couldn't reach them, I called my father. I never said what I was feeling, but sensing something wrong, he talked gently, urging me to go out or drive up to the country. I called him several times that summer. "Oh Marjorie, I was just thinking of you," he'd say. "How are you dear? What're you doing today?"

I knew it was time to go back into treatment. When I first got to New York, I tried to look up Easser but she'd died years before of cancer while still a young woman. I talked to my friends and they suggested Lillian Malcove, a training analyst at the New York

Psychoanalytic, the most Freudian of the Institutes. I called her, and she agreed to see me for a consultation.

I went to see her on a cloudy afternoon right after labor day. She was a small lively woman who made seventy seem elegant.

"Why did you marry so soon?" she asked at the end of our first session. "Don't make the same mistake now." I walked out feeling confident and hopeful.

I assumed Malcove would treat me, but at our last session she seemed to be preparing to refer me out. "Aren't you going to see me?" I asked.

"I'd like to, but I think you'll need treatment for two or three years and I'm not sure I'll still be working. Look, the last thing you need is another loss." She smiled a warm smile that made me feel she did want to work with me, and suggested I see a Dr. Frank. He'd been a student of hers. She said he was intuitive and understanding.

I saw him once and found his questions insulting.

"Of course you can't see him when you feel like that," Malcove said, when I called her. "I thought you two would hit it off. I'll give you other names, let me know what happens. Only work with someone who makes you comfortable."

I took the names, but I was too disappointed to see anyone else.

One good thing came out of that summer: Frieda met a man she liked, Jerry Wiener, at a Medical School reunion party. Jerry was a pediatrician with a big practice, a solid reputation, and an intense desire to be with Frieda. They stopped by unexpectedly on a Saturday morning, Frieda striking in a white pants suit lighter than her skin. Over the years I'd seen her with a number of men, and they were all tall, dark, and too handsome, the kind of man who was continually checking his smile in mirrors or car windows. The man Frieda pulled through my door was short, round, with blue eyes, white hair and a happy expression — Santa without the beard. I found it hard to see them as a couple, but Frieda reached for Jerry's hand, placing her head against his shoulder.

Jerry was always at Frieda's. They both made me feel welcome, but it was different. I didn't get to spend much time alone with Frieda, and didn't want to become a third wheel. I went up for dinner one evening late in August, and ended up talking about my trouble living alone that summer.

"What's to be so upset about?" Jerry asked, accentuating his Jewish accent. "I can't live alone either. Until Frieda came along I'd go home with a different woman every night. I'd wake at two in the morning not knowing whose house I was in, or where the bathroom was. That's how I am — I accept it."

I liked the way Jerry was so open, and understood better why Frieda was so drawn to him.

Frieda had one analysis, a series of relationships that didn't drive her crazy, and was settling down with Jerry. By contrast, I had just about as many therapists as I had lovers, and neither quite worked out. The luck of the draw I'd tell myself, but I knew, although vaguely, that my problems with therapy and men were related and they were caused by me. If I'd followed Malcove's suggestions, I'd already be in treatment working on myself. Frieda had worked on not being so drawn to such handsome, stuck-on-themselves men and ended up with Jerry.

Chapter 20. Mom

Before we returned from California my parents had sold their house in Brooklyn, and spent their winters in Ft. Lauderdale and their summers in the Adirondacks. But where ever they were I got a call every Sunday morning. Then late one Sunday night in March, my mother called again.

"Don't worry," she said. "Your father had a small stroke, but everything's going to be fine. I just saw him in the hospital. He's the same old Oscar. He can think and walk and talk. He can yell at me too."

My father had collapsed at a United Jewish Appeal dinner, and the paramedics took him to Florida Medical Center. I called Ved Gupta, my father's doctor, but couldn't reach him. Then I called Continental and booked a morning flight to Ft. Lauderdale. I kept calling the hospital, and finally got a nurse on my father's floor. She was reassuring — a tiny bleed, no real danger. The next morning another nurse said he was even better.

That afternoon, feeling relieved, I drove past the high bubbly fountain at the entrance to Woodlands, the community where my parents lived, and headed to their smallish green house that backed onto the golf course. The front door was unlocked, so I walked in and called to my mother.

She was in the kitchen, her back against the sink, a faded blue apron around her waist, a cigarette in her hand.

"Mom, I'm here."

She looked up. "I didn't even hear you. I'm so deaf these days. When people call to ask about Oscar I hear buzzing and say 'fine, fine.'" She wiped her hands on her apron and hugged me. We stood together for a long time, holding hands.

"How's it going?" I said. "You saw Dad this morning?"

"He bawled me out for telling you. Said it wasn't serious enough." She laughed, making a shrill sound. "But why am I standing here like this? Lunch? Tea? I baked you some Mandelbrot. Mandelbrot and tea?"

"Sure. Can I help?"

"No, go put your things away. You know I like to putter when I'm nervous."

Small scarlet flowers bloomed on the sides of my mother's cup. Her lips were thin and pale, and her uncombed hair looked brittle. I'd never seen her look so old, and put my hand on her arm.

"You'll talk to the doctor, Margie," she said, looking at me with frightened eyes. "You'll find out everything and tell me the truth?"

"Of course. But Dr. Gupta's telling you the truth. I called the hospital last night and this morning. It was a small bleed just like he said."

My mother sighed and sat nodding her head. Then she looked off the way she did when I was younger and she'd be thinking about her own mother. I hadn't seen her do that in years.

"Didn't Dr. Gupta say the stroke came from hypertension?" I prompted.

"Yes, he's lowering Oscar's pressure right now. He has to go slow. He says it's been high for years. I made appointments for him with Dr. Gupta, but you know your father."

I did know my father. "Stay away from doctors and lawyers," was one of his favorite comments.

After finishing her tea, my mother went to take a nap. She left her door part way open. That made me feel tender toward her, like she was my child.

When she came back out, she looked better. The deep lines on her face were gone, and her hair looked softer. She'd dressed in a pink flowered outfit with big white button earrings and low-heeled, sandals. Her hips were full and she stood erect, but a narrowing, a frailness, was settling in around her neck and shoulders.

We got our passes and went upstairs in a small elevator. Dad was sitting up in bed, arguing politics with a red bearded man. My father introduced everyone, then my mother pulled the curtain separating the beds.

"You heard what I a jackass I made of myself," my father said in greeting. "If I'd seen Dr. Gupta even once, none of this would've happened. I ended up keeling over with five hundred people watching." He pursed his lips, and shook his head. "What a mess. "

Mom sat forward, her thin eyebrows raised. "Oscar, did you pledge before you fell over?"

"No. I don't think so."

"See, right there we saved money. That's good."

"And if I passed on, would you be happy with those savings?"

"No, funeral expenses are much too high. Besides, who would I yell at?"

Dad reached to touch Mom's face. She thrust it toward him. "Lakila, Lakila," he said, cradling her chin with his fingers. "You'll be making your best jokes on my deathbed." He turned to me. "Your mother's some character."

I nodded.

Before we left my mother put clean handkerchiefs and pajamas in my father's dresser drawer, packed his dirty laundry in a brown bag, and announced, "I'm in the mood for fried shrimp."

The next day Dr. Gupta called to say my father had an arrhythmia, and needed an operation for a pacemaker. I called Beth Israel and arranged to use some vacation time. I had to be there.

A few days later Dad came home and lots of people started dropping by. While dabbling in Florida politics, my father was appointed Councilman in Tamarac to complete someone's term. He liked the work, ran for re-election, and got so many votes he became Vice Mayor of Tamarac. His term was over, but he was still involved in local politics, so he had plenty of political buddies who came trooping over.

Mom took charge of the visiting, limiting it to the afternoons. She greeted the guests, kept the conversations going and said goodbye when she felt it was time. I answered the phone, did the shopping, served the guests, and took my father's pulse before he swallowed his meds. During the day I was busy, but after my parents went to sleep, I'd sit reading or watching TV. I felt edgy and lonely. They were getting older, and it made me want to flee.

Chapter 21. Sternbach

Back in New York I was eager to throw myself into my work, but as much as I liked Beth Israel, I knew I couldn't get my research done there. It was a small department, already involved in one major project. Reluctantly, I began to look for openings at other hospitals. Ted Sokoloff, a medical school classmate now at Mt. Sinai, called to say that their chief of Outpatient Psychiatry had left, and that their chairman, Manny Sternbach, was eager to fill the position by July, before the next wave of residents arrived.

I'd seen Emmanuel Sternbach and heard him lecture. He was a brilliant man with an unusual background, a biological researcher with analytic training. I sent him my resume and he called me for an interview.

Purposely, I arrived early to wander around the hospital. I'd interned at Sinai, but that was before it acquired the medical school and became a major teaching center. As the appointment time grew closer I checked the Valium in my pocket, and headed for Sternbach's office. I entered through an adjacent room that had a couple of wooden tables, straight-backed wooden chairs, and a coffee setup with a sign saying, "Pay fifty cents." Beyond that was the inner office where a woman with short gray hair sat typing, occasionally scratching at her head. I introduced myself.

Barely looking up, she said, "I'm Sally, Dr. Sternbach's secretary. He's expecting you, but he's with someone right now. Just wait out there." She pointed to the tables and chairs.

I sat looking around wondering what it would be like to work here now. Back when I'd interned, they had experts in almost every field, doctors came in at two a.m. to see their patients, and at midnight they put out giant platters of corned beef and pastrami for the house staff. It still had the experts, probably more, but I'd heard all these jokes about back stabbing being the most frequent surgical procedure. I also knew that all major teaching hospitals were famous for politics and double-dealing, and that I'd reached a level where ugly politics couldn't be avoided.

Behind Sally was a sunny window filled with large blooming cactus plants. I was admiring them when a hefty bearded man in a long white coat came rushing out of Sternbach's office, blushing to the tips of his ears. Behind him a voice boomed, "Pay for your coffee! Who the hell do you think you are?"

"Dr. Raskin's here," Sally said, looking up.

Sternbach came striding toward me, his hand extended. He was a dapper man with beautifully cut gray hair, a large wide nose that gave him a generous look, and keen brown eyes. "Sorry about all the ruckus, but I'm sure you figured out that wasn't about coffee. And speaking of coffee, would you like some?"

I quickly wiped my palm on my skirt and shook his hand. "No, thanks, I'm fine." Caffeine was the last thing I needed.

He led me through his office to a large round glass coffee table with a brass rim, surrounded by four green chairs. We sat on opposite sides of the table.

"That argument was about excellence," he said. "Or more to the point, the erosion of excellence. Do you think a first-rate doctor becomes a hack overnight? No, it starts out with little things. My wife took our daughter to the pediatrician because of a sore throat. He didn't take a culture and wanted to treat her with antibiotics. I switched doctors. I try to run an excellent department here, so I pick up all the little things. I'm sure they talk about it. Probably call me Captain Queeg and a whole lot worse."

He was smiling in this confiding way, his eyes fixed on mine. He seemed to be saying you and I understand. You know what it takes to run a good department. You know all I have to go through. I felt flattered, special, close to the man.

He told me he found my recommendations impressive. We talked about California, then, putting on half glasses, he said, "You've never run a whole outpatient department. Now that concerns me."

I'd been anticipating that question. "It's my next step, and I'm ready to take it. I called some people here to see how your program is set up. I'd like to change the whole arrangement. I'd like to merge the psychotherapy and medication clinics, and create teams. I'd have caseload supervision as well as special supervisors." I went on to detail my ideas about team meetings, case conferences, intake, discharge, right down to how I'd change the forms in the chart.

Sternbach sat listening, the back of his head against his chair.

"Well, that sounds good to me."

He opened the manila folder that had copies of my papers inside. He said anxiety was an interesting topic, and asked if I planned to continue working on it. I told him I did. He nodded, then slid one of my papers toward me, his finger on a paragraph, "Where did you get this social rating scale?"

"I adapted it."

"And you tested it for reliability and validity?"

"Yes, I could show you the results another time."

He sat back for a long moment with his eyes half closed. I watched him, feeling excited.

He opened his eyes and asked, "Do you know my work?"

"Of course."

"There's no 'of course' about it. Half the doctors in this department have no idea what I do. It's actually quite frightening in a way. But if we do work out this job, and so far it looks like we will, how would you like to join my research staff?"

"I'd be honored." I had a quick flash of a headline on the front page of *The New York Times* reading 'Psychiatrist wins Nobel Prize," and buried in the article would be my name. Who knows maybe there'd be a picture of the team too. I felt giddy, but then more realistic thoughts filtered in. I was agreeing to run a large outpatient

142

department that included an emergency room. I would have to do work for the department and the hospital; that was always part of it. I planned to do my own research, and now I was agreeing to work on his.

Sternbach sat watching me, tapping his pencil on the table.

"I'm afraid I'm biting off too much," I said.

"That's an important issue. I would've been disappointed if you hadn't raised it. Take six months, maybe nine, make your outpatient program work, than step back and let it run itself. Once the program runs itself you're home free. You keep smoothing things out, putting in appearances. That'll take you what — eight, ten hours a week?"

I didn't know how to answer. Programs treated with that kind of neglect always failed. And he knew that. "But I have to stay involved with my own program."

He folded his glasses and held them. "You know Dr. Raskin. It takes a very special kind of person to be an academic. Maybe you'd be happier going into private practice and coming here to do a few hours of resident supervision. Or, you could put a few hours into research. It's the life most psychiatrists lead." He smiled. "Not many are doomed to academia, although it takes them a while to see it."

I felt angry and confused. I paused, then said, "I'm not here to talk about my career choice. I've already made that. We're arguing about how much time it would take to keep a good program going."

His smile was bigger than ever. "That's a good answer. Why don't we just see how it goes."

I nodded. I wasn't sure exactly what had happened.

"Of course, you'll come to our Senior Staff meetings where all the big decisions are made. You'll be the first woman to attend. Now I have a theory that one good woman can change the chemistry of the group. Wake up the men."

That seemed a bizarre expectation, and I thought about it as he filled me in on other meetings. Then he said, "Oh, one more thing. You'll take part in our medical school teaching. The women need role models. Just give a few lectures."

I felt knocked off balance. I squeezed the Valium in my pocket, hoping that somehow I was absorbing some through my fingers.

"I'm not a good lecturer," I said, remembering Ruesch's words. "But I do well with smaller groups. I'd be happy to teach in the clerkship."

"Strange. You look like you'd be a good lecturer. The clerkship's fine, but that'll take more of your time."

He stood and shook my hand. "Any last minute questions?"

Chapter 22. At Sinai

When I arrived at Sinai in July outpatient was a mess. The two psychiatrists who'd worked with the previous chief had just left, so the twenty-four residents training there, each treating over twenty patients regularly and evaluating new cases weekly, had mostly supervision on the run. They were understandably overwhelmed and angry. I put in fourteen-hour days, but it was impossible for me to supervise each resident, cover the ER, and back the residents by phone each night. I was running ads in the *New York Times* for new staff, but meanwhile the person helping most was Alvin Bloch. He was the doctor who'd dashed out of Sternbach's office before my interview, propelled by accusations of chiseling coffee. He was also vice chairman of the department and Sternbach's closest buddy.

I'd be up to see Sternbach each day to find other psychiatrists to help. At first he asked for volunteers, but no one came forward. Then after I'd been there a couple of weeks, he said, "I spent the entire weekend thinking about this problem. Rhoda, my wife — the woman has wonderful instincts — couldn't believe no one volunteered. 'Outrageous,' Rhoda said. And she's right. Driving to work this morning I began thinking about all the doctors here who don't pull their weight." He pulled an envelope from his shirt pocket. "I jotted some names down. I thought we'd go through them together. I'll simply order people to help."

He read a list so long it sounded like he was naming his entire department. I'd learned by then that he overstated things to make his point, but real feelings were at the heart of each overstatement.

"I'm sure you're asking yourself why I keep these people on," Sternbach said, stretching his legs out and loosening his tie. "Well, I'm asking myself the same question." He looked at his list. "But see, in each case there's a good reason. Take Carp, he's first. The man's had two heart attacks, he's sending a son through medical school, a daughter through some graduate program, and he won't get work anywhere else. He's been here longer than I have. I have to be loyal, right? But how long should I stay loyal to people who aren't loyal back? Now that's not a trivial question."

Before he could answer himself, I said, "Is Carp someone who could help? Maybe supervise some residents? That's not too taxing."

Sternbach leaned forward, his eyes shining. "You're starting fresh. The residents are excited by all the changes. They're excited by you! Why have your service associated with a broken down man who can't make decisions. Carp has no push, no oomph. I don't think he gets it up at home. Told me once he thought his wife was playing around."

Each day we worked our way further down the list, Sternbach deciding each doctor wasn't fit to help after confiding the most intimate details of the man's life. I was intrigued, but also disturbed to hear these secrets about people in my own department. I told myself that ordinarily Sternbach kept such stories to himself, but was confiding in me because it was an unusual situation and I such an understanding person.

In early August I found a psychiatrist I wanted to hire, James Boyer. At first Sternbach opposed him because he wasn't academic enough — hadn't written any papers, but Bloch interceded, saying he couldn't keep putting so much time in outpatient. A few weeks later I found another psychiatrist, Charlie Kolton. This time Sternbach didn't say a word. Bloch interviewed the man and he was hired. With these two men on board, my service was set. I could run things the way I wanted.

It was fall by then, the air was clear and made me think of apples. People strode down the street in woolen jackets, bright scarves tossed round their necks. At Sinai the doctors stepped more briskly, their white coats looked extra starched, and everywhere crisp sheets of paper announced new classes, new lectures, new meetings.

Sternbach's research meetings began in November. When I got to the first one, three people were already there: two biologists and Bloch, who had just joined the project. Alvin Bloch was a big man with a large round face, curly dark hair that reached around his chin to form a short beard, and a deep chest that drifted into a large soft belly. Some people thought he looked cuddly, like a big bear, but I was put off by his small greedy eyes.

Sternbach began by detailing the nature of his work. He studied the biology of mood, and this particular study, long in progress, was on depression. I'd read the reprints he sent me, and it was exciting to hear him talk about his work and realize I'd be part of it. From what I gathered, his grant, like most those days, was under-funded. He spent his money on the biologists who measured hormones, and relied on volunteers — like Bloch and me — to do the rest. At the end of the meeting he said he needed more subjects, or more precisely, more blood from depressed patients. He wanted early morning samples from patients on the wards, and suggested Bloch and I split the time. After the meeting I went to Bloch's office to make arrangements. Bloch tried to get me to do most of the work claiming he'd put in so much time at outpatient already. I countered that he was helping the department, not me. After a bit of staring back and forth he agreed to do his share. I left with an uncomfortable feeling.

I walked down to the first floor and saw Isabel, chief of psychiatric social work and a new friend, standing near my office. I pulled her inside and told her what happened.

"He's just a bully," she said, sitting down. "It's good you spoke up." Tall, with weathered skin and hooded gray eyes, Isabel gave off the sense of having mellowed after a good bit of living. She was wearing silver earrings the size of quarters that balanced her strong jaw. I assumed she grew into her looks because she seemed unaware she was attractive. Widowed young with a son away in college, she rarely talked about her marriage or her relationships with men. Her mind was often on an operation for breast cancer, an apparently successful one she'd had three year before. She was straightforward and loyal and had an unusual attitude about hospital work: she did more than her share, claiming doing it was easier than fighting about it.

After my confrontation with Bloch, I was apprehensive at Sternbach's research meetings, but the sessions I came to dread were those of Steering Committee; that's where I was supposed to change the chemistry of the group. Everyone seemed quiet there, and I wasn't sure why. Then at the beginning of our third meeting, Sternbach stormed in, his face puffed and purple. The room fell silent and everyone sat lower in his chair as Sternbach stalked around us, panther-like, saying a psychiatrist in this room had made comments at a hospital meeting that made him look foolish with a dean. Everyone slouched further, including me. We went to numerous hospital meetings, and said many things that taken out of context could've upset him. Anyone of us might be the culprit. Still circling, Sternbach announced, "Those foolish words could come only from someone loose-mouthed, careless and stupid." He let that sink in, then stopped and stared directly at Dr. Habib, a young man who was acting head of child psychiatry. Dr. Habib turned white, his Adam's apple bobbed in his throat. Sternbach said the meeting was over, and the rest of us moved quickly from the room. I never found out what Habib said, or how Sternbach found out. But that was part of the pattern — you never knew when the flood was coming, or who'd go down in it.

Yet I felt relatively safe. My outpatient department was flourishing, the two new doctors worked out well. Patient care was good, and the residents were vocal about liking the service. Sternbach kept complimenting me, or repeating compliments he'd heard about me. The residents and social workers took an interest in my anxiety work, and a few were eager to treat anxious patients. With their help I set up Mt. Sinai's first anxiety clinic. We used psychotherapy, medications, and behavioral approaches like graded exposure for phobias, and had some major successes. I even arranged a Grand Rounds where Boyer, Kolton, and a couple of the residents presented some of our more challenging cases.

In late June each service gave a farewell-to-the-residents party. Sternbach and Bloch made the rounds together. We'd set a buffet table in a closed section of the lobby, and music came from a boom box on a chair. Bloch, wearing a blue suit and red bow tie, drank, ate, and danced with the prettiest residents and social workers. Sternbach, dressed in tones of gray, talked briefly with each resident, then stood nursing his drink.

I went over to him and said, "It must be hard showing up at so many parties."

He looked at me strangely, as if I were getting too personal. I smiled and backed off. I was hurt, but figured he had something on his mind.

As it turned out, it was the first sign that Sternbach was changing toward me. He didn't seem angry, but it was worse, he acted more and more like I didn't exist. At first I thought I was making it up, but there was no eye contact in meetings, no chats in the hall, no smiles at jokes I made.

I had weekly lunches with Isabel at Teachers, a Sinai hangout on Madison Avenue. The menu chalked on a blackboard, never changed, yet Isabel read it through every time. After deciding she wanted a grilled chicken salad, I told her about Sternbach's coldness.

"Well, he's a strange man," she said, her chin on her fist. "When I was in the hospital he came to see me before my operation. He was a delight, he was helpful, but later he never asked how I was." She looked at me and shrugged. "I was hurt. But new psychiatrists always talk about falling in and out of favor with him for no reason. He's that kind of person. It's his problem not ours."

I nodded, then changed the subject to the trip to Tuscany Isabel would be taking in August. I listened to the places she'd be staying, but kept wondering if her explanation about Sternbach was right. I'd thought I had a special closeness to him.

One morning, I saw Bloch having breakfast in the hospital cafeteria. He was eating a jelly donut and appeared in a good mood. I joined him and said, "Sternbach's acting different with me. Is he angry?"

Bloch licked his fingers. "Probably disappointed, but look kid, he gets disappointed with everyone. He had great hopes about you. Thought you'd give a big speech that everyone quoted. Or write a ground-breaking paper. He always goes through this, then he forgets his big expectations and things are fine again."

I smiled, but felt bad. I'd never give a big speech everyone would quote; I wouldn't give any speech. It would take a while before I had data for a paper, and I doubted it would be ground breaking. Old doubts about my competence swelled up in me, and I wanted to get back in Sternbach's good graces. I held some special seminars for residents and sent Sternbach an invitation. He didn't come. When it was his birthday I gave him a bottle of Courvoisier. He voiced a disinterested thank you. I realized that I'd never been special to him.

Now I became fair game for scapegoating by Sternbach or Bloch, and found myself continually fighting to keep my service intact. Each visit to a departmental meeting tightened the knot in my stomach.

Chapter 23. Aikido

One evening during my second winter at Sinai, I saw a group of people on Fifth Avenue near Tenth Street who radiated so much happiness and pleasure I wondered what could make them feel so good. I tried to walk by them whenever I could, and from bits of their conversation, learned they were from the Aikido School in a nearby building. Later, sitting at a wooden table at the Jefferson Market Library, I read about Aikido, a Japanese martial art designed to promote peace. Aikido students learned to be strong, calm, alert, and to use their opponent's energy against them. I looked at the pictures of confident men in black and white outfits throwing their enemies to the floor with a turn of the wrist. The founder, Uyeshiba, was said to have thrown his with just a look. It would be a useful talent at Sinai, but apart from that fantasy, Aikido appealed to me. There was something there I wanted to learn, but could I start a martial art at forty-seven? I was not a terrifically well-coordinated forty-seven either.

A few weeks later Ali and I walked passed the building just as the Aikido group was leaving. I watched closely as they stood talking under the streetlights. Most were in their twenties, but a few looked my age. The Japanese couple who came out last, an attractive pair in brown leather jackets, seemed well into their forties. I went up to the building, and in the doorway, found a container full of leaflets with class times. On the back they said: Visitors Always Welcome.

151

"Try it," Ali urged. "If you like it, I'll come too. You know, it would be good for you to try new things."

The next night I visited class and watched smiling people in black and white outfits throwing each other to the floor. The ivory white room was filled by a huge rectangular mat, except at the front where a row of wooden chairs and a desk stood before high windows. On the desk, purple irises rose out of a ceramic vase. A student asked if he could help me, then pointed to one of the chairs. The Japanese man I'd seen outside was leading the group. He was the teacher, Sensei Eotio. In his white top and full black trousers, he looked impressive. He called out something in Japanese, and the students knelt before him, knees apart, backs straight. Squatting before his students, he pushed each lightly on the chest. I was surprised to see that most fell over. They got right back in position, asked to be tested again, and often stayed upright with the second push. All of this was done seriously, but with good humor. When I saw that even the clumsy students seemed encouraged, I signed up.

At my first session I felt as if I was entering a new country with its own rules and language. I stuffed my socks into my shoes and lined them up in front with the others. With my toes pressing into the mat, I buoyantly strode to the women's dressing room. It was small and smelled of sweat and powder. The few women inside said a quick hello, as I changed into my *gi* — white cotton pants and a heavy white jacket secured by a thick, white belt. When I came back out, feeling pleased but a little foolish, the Japanese woman I'd seen before was waiting. She told me she was Miho, Sensei's wife, and one of the teachers. She looked tall in her white top and black trousers, although standing next to her, I realized she was less than five feet. Miho had an oval face, short black hair and smelled of tangerines.

At exactly five after the hour, Sensei stood with twenty of us facing him, in two rows. First, we all repeated an oath about seeking peace, and part of it was a promise to do good in secret. I liked the oath, and I liked saying it out loud with the others. An hour of exercises came next. Miho tapped me on the shoulder during certain ones and said, "Watch." Then she stood beside me explaining the movements.

After a five-minute rest, Aikido started. It was done with partners, and Miho was mine. Sensei demonstrated the first technique with Audrey, the assistant teacher, a pale plump woman who came alive before us, her eyes flashing green. When Sensei called out *shomen-uchi*, Audrey flew at him, her blond hair streaming, her arm speeding sword-like toward his head. Sensei stepped forward, caught her arm — one hand near the wrist and the other at her shoulder. Using her arm as a lever, he circled her around and down to the mat. She bounced back up and bowed. Then, they reversed positions, and went through it again with Audrey pinning Sensei. In Aikido the attacker always loses.

When Sensei called out *"shomen-uchi"* to the group, I raised my arm in imitation of Audrey.

"Not yet," Miho said. "First you learn fall right. More important."

I watched as she crossed one foot behind the other and rolled back softly a few times. When it was my turn, I fell back stiffly, making a thwacking sound. It hurt a little, and the sound was embarrassing. It was the loudest noise in the room. I kept trying but continued to fall back heavily.

Miho said, "Stop and rest."

Sensei came toward us. "Sometimes hard to relax," he said. "New Yorkers have big trouble. Always up in head. Make you tense, fall over easy." He placed his hands over his head like a waiter carrying a heavy tray, then walked in different directions, swaying alarmingly with each step. "That you," he said. "Must move center down." He placed his hand, palm down, near his forehead and pressed it slowly to right below his navel, gaining balance as he did this.

"Take long time," he said, laughing. "Took me twenty years." I liked his laugh.

I spent that entire session rolling backwards. And I did get better. I relaxed some, allowing my back to curve. That made it hurt less and the sound was softer. Miho was extraordinarily patient, and when Sensei said relaxing was hard, I felt he understood me. When I was a teenager taking dance classes, the teacher would order me to relax, and I'd go spastic.

I went to class three times a week. If I missed a session, I got a headache or an aching shoulder and felt tense. Meanwhile, things at work were even more unpleasant. Budgets were shrinking, a couple of psychiatrists were laid off, and Sternbach and Bloch were scapegoating someone new each week. Changes were coming at home too. With a bit of worry in his voice, Keith told me that he wanted to go to college at Berkeley to be near his father. I agreed, knowing it would be good for him, but I also knew I'd be lonely without him. I had half a dozen friends to help me if something went wrong, but there were only a few people I could call to get a bite or go to a movie. Something surprising had happened: all my unmarried New York friends who wanted a partner had found one. Frieda had married Jerry. Jane, a friend from Beth Israel, had met a divorced lawyer through friends, and they were living together. Tess, a nurse and an old friend from Medical School days, married an old high school flame.

In many ways Aikido was like therapy. I was learning to change patterns I didn't know I had, and did it by correcting the same mistakes over and over. At almost every session, Miho gave me pointers. She kept showing me that I stopped breathing when I got tense. Holding your breath is common in anxiety; it makes the symptoms worse. I began making conscious efforts to keep my breathing slow and regular, to stand straighter and keep my center down. And it did make me feel more confident.

Joe, a black belt, an Italian from Brooklyn, began practicing with me.

"You remind me of myself," he said right away. "I mess up by trying too hard too."

Joe was accomplished at Aikido, but nowhere as good as Miho. Her arms were like thick young vines, but Joe was tense at times, making his grip brittle. Sensei taught that strength came out of relaxation.

After Aikido practice a group often went out to eat. On weekends Sensei and Miho came along. It was a nice bit of social life. Sensei shyly talked about sports or Aikido, Miho liked hearing jokes and bits of gossip. When we went to eat, Joe usually walked beside me. He was different from most people I knew — a former juvenile delinquent, reformed and computer educated, courtesy of the Marines. He had the face of an altar boy (he'd been one), and a habit of sucking in his almost non-existent gut, flexing his well-muscled arm and saying, "not bad for an old man." We were the same age, and he had a breezy way of flirting that made me feel attractive.

In May, my name was on the list of people who had to take Aikido tests. I pictured myself standing in front of the group in my *gi,* graceful as Frankenstein, then running off the mat in a panic. I thought of telling Sensei I wasn't ready, but before I could say anything he announced that testing was part of our training. Next weekend, Audrey would open the training hall, the *dojo* they called it, in the mornings so we could practice. Joe said to come Saturday morning. He'd help.

When I went to practice on Saturday, about ten students, all at different levels and a few black belts, were on the mat stretching. Audrey sat at Sensei's desk, her blond hair piled on her head, writing. She could teach well, but most of us hesitated to ask her. She came out of a dance background, and her corrections were often harsh. Joe, in his Aikido outfit, squatted on the floor, drinking coffee from a paper cup.

As we went slowly through my test, Joe corrected my major mistakes. Then we went through it quickly over and over until I could do the moves without thinking.

At times, I'd find my sweating body pressed against his. To be sure practice didn't become sexual, any suggestive remarks or gestures could get you thrown out of the *dojo* for good. Joe must've learned well because he never seemed aroused when he practiced with me. But I hadn't learned it: when his arm brushed my breast or his breath reached my neck, I felt a tingling in my groin.

"I'd ask you to lunch," Joe said after practice. "But I promised to do some work for Audrey. And remember, you're doing great." He flashed his boyish smile.

I went to lunch with some female students, including Judy, a married doctoral student who was the *dojo*'s best gossip. We walked to Swensen's on Fourth and Mercer, and over rare hamburgers and malteds, Judy brought the conversation around to Joe.

"I like him," Patty, one of the new students said. "He's cute."

"Sure, he's cute," Judy answered, spooning up her malted. "And he knows it. He uses it. He's been sleeping with Audrey for years and with other students too."

"Doesn't Audrey object?" Patty asked, her round face flushed.

I pushed my plate away to show my lack of interest.

"Who knows? They keep their affair a secret. Maybe they get a kick out of the whole *a trois* thing." Judy looked at me. "You're the psychiatrist, don't you think it's sick?"

"It does sound weird."

Walking home, the flowerbeds around the trees were overflowing with tulips and daffodils. I felt out of phase with the season.

On the day of the test I was shaky but didn't take a Valium. It didn't seem right, when the training was all about learning to relax yourself. I tried to watch the other students' tests, but found myself focusing on a small bald spot at the back of Sensei's head. I felt cut off from the others, as if a strong wind was blowing past my head. When my name was called I rushed up, bowed to Miho, my partner, then to Sensei. He called out words and I moved half in a trance, giving myself a pep talk, *just focus, take a good deep breath, you're not that dizzy.* Before I knew it, Miho and I were bowing to each other, and bowing again to Sensei.

"Pass," he said.

Suddenly my whole body felt loose and light. I'd done it! That was more exciting than passing. My next test would be better. I'd be calmer. I could feel changes in my body already. Sensei and Miho and the other students kept telling me my step was lighter, and my grip softer. I saw changes in the other students too.

I thanked Miho in the dressing room, but Joe wasn't around.

When I got downstairs, I found him standing outside, the hood of a gray sweatshirt pulled over his head, smoking. His mouth was curled open, and a fleck of paper stuck to his lower lip.

"That was great. Really terrific. Want to celebrate — how bout dinner tonight? A drink?"

"Maybe another time," I said in a detached way, trying to convey there'd be no other time. I didn't want to make a mess in my new haven.

156

Joe made a show of looking disappointed. I shrugged and left.

After I passed my test, Ali joined the *dojo*. She came mostly on Saturdays. She was the youngest in class, twelve years old, and she was good, her movements easy. Sensei and Miho took a special liking to her. Sensei taught her a different Japanese phrase each week, as well as Origami. He worked with her a lot. Miho worked with her too, and picked her partners, only the gentlest of black belts. I liked having Ali in the class, and felt it was good for her too. There were no men around New York trying to teach her things, praising her. Sensei and Miho wrote to her when she was in San Francisco. She made the cake for Sensei's birthday.

Joe liked Ali, and when she was around he never flirted with me. But he asked me out, a couple of times more, joking, "It's your last chance." I'd smile, pleased by his attention, and pleased even more that we managed to just stay friends.

Chapter 24. My Forty Eighth Birthday

I started my third year at Sinai in July, 1983, a summer so hot and steamy that people in the streets looked like they were sleepwalking. With my kids back in California, I kept myself busy. At the *dojo,* I helped paint the peeling white walls and patched torn spots on the mat. I spent a week in the Hamptons with Frieda and Jerry. On weekend nights, I saw Isabel.

In the fall — although my kids were back — I kept getting tenser. Budget cuts increased, and the Senior Staff Meetings exploded into war zones. One evening in late September I was sitting in my apartment with Isabel, complaining about Sinai. She listened, sliding her silver bangles up her arm and allowing them to clink back together.

"You have to stop wrinkling your forehead," she said. "You're getting a big crease there."

I laughed and smoothed my forehead with my fingers.

"Seriously, you have to learn to protect yourself more. Men seem to take these things better."

I was both annoyed and flattered by her concern. "Well, what do think I should do? Take testosterone? I am in Aikido."

Isabel reached over and touched my arm. "Marge, you need more than Aikido."

"That again. Look, Iz, I have a complicated, mostly disappointing, treatment history. Do you want me to repeat it therapist by therapist?"

"No." Isabel smoothed her skirt as she stood. "You know I'm right."

She was right. But just talking about treatment brought back that tick in the back of my throat that came before a panic. I taught that treatment helped with anxiety, and I'd seen it work in my own patients and the resident's cases, but, on a gut level that wipes out reason, I knew it wouldn't help me. Dr. Easser had leaned forward, her hair curling under her chin, as she told me I had trouble looking at my deeper feeling. If I'd looked at my feelings toward Michael sooner, my marriage would've ended before I was ready. But why couldn't I look at my feelings when I was losing Philip? Philip had said he wasn't angry any more, that I'd done what I had to. He learned about it in his own analysis after his mother died, when he almost bled to death. A bleed to protest her going. Attachment lodged in flesh. Don't give up, he said. What was I afraid of seeing now? I had no husband, no boyfriend, my job wasn't secure, I wasn't the world's best mother. Would I see myself as someone without love, who worked only to please, a core of rage decked out in silks and linens?

What if I started counting on another therapist who turned away, said, "Sorry can't help, we're just too different?"

No, I'd count on myself, Aikido, and my trusty blue Valium tablets.

By the end of September, Medical School was in full swing, and Bloch and Sternbach were studying each service. Most of the unit chiefs were complaining about them walking into meetings unannounced. Since Bloch held a weekly case conference in outpatient I was hoping we'd be spared, but one morning Sternbach and Bloch came in and sat down as I was interviewing a patient in front of my team. I could see them out of the corner of my eye. While I was listening to the patient, a young woman with mild depression, my hands started sweating.

Unlike me, the woman seemed undisturbed by the newcomers. She said, "Sorry. I didn't quite understand your last question."

I looked at her. I couldn't remember what I'd asked. My throat was closing, my heart was pounding. I felt a full blown panic coming.

The woman leaned forward. She was pale with straight blond hair, and her eyes blinked nervously. "I'm sorry," she repeated. "I didn't understand your question."

Her nervousness calmed me.

"I'm sorry too," I said, feeling myself again. "You know, I forgot my own question."

We both laughed and I went on with the interview. Later, Bloch told me they'd been pleased with the conference, thought I'd covered all the bases, but as I walked to my office, my legs felt shaky.

Rosh ha-Shanah was early that year. Keith, Ali and I celebrated at home. I made veal stew over noodles, asparagus vinaigrette, and bought chocolate chip cookies. At the end of the meal, we dipped apple slices in a dish of dark honey and wished each other a sweet New Year. I told Keith he should do that next year when he was away at Berkeley. He laughed.

I looked at him. He was handsome with open clean-cut features, a high-bridged nose, and rosy cheeks. I felt chills. What would it be like without him? Would time speed up until Ali went away, too? I didn't want to think about that. Or about the contact lens that was stuck in my eye until Keith placed the side of my head in a bowl of water, and the contact floated out. Or, about the mice that paraded around our stovetop at night, until Keith stuffed up the holes in the wall with steel wool. Or, about how much I counted on him to listen to my problems. Get a grip on yourself. You run a big department. You've passed three Aikido tests. Stand tall. Find your center.

Keith was holding an apple slice over the dish of honey. He looked concerned. "When did you last see Isabel?" he asked.

"Yesterday."

"Well, maybe you want to call her, or Frieda?"

"Oh, I'm fine." I didn't want him to worry about how I'd manage without him, so I hummed as I cleared the dishes. From then on, I tried to reassure Keith and Ali by going out every Saturday night. If I wasn't meeting a friend, I'd take myself to a movie. I made efforts to appear high spirited and happy.

My forty-eighth birthday was coming in early October. On the weekend before it, there were Psychiatry Boards in New York City. I was an examiner, which meant I questioned candidates about the video of a patient they'd just seen, then rated their answers. I'd done it before and liked it. It was a big event, a chance to keep up on what was happening, and see former teachers, classmates, and students who came in from all over the country. Hundreds of doctors would be there. Divorce rates being what they were, I thought, well, maybe here.

On Friday I had an appointment for a makeover at Elizabeth Arden, my birthday present to myself. In a small room under flattering lights, a man with a European accent studied me. He covered my face with foundation rubbed on with a sponge, and brought out my cheekbones with two blushers, one brighter than the other. After painting a base coat from my eyelashes to my eyebrows, he brushed my eyelids with copper shadow. "Keep it interesting," he murmured, starting on my lips. Before I left he looked at me with approval, and highlighted my face with golden powder. I walked through that red door half expecting some attractive man to rush over and insist we get together. I walked down Fifth Avenue thinking I fit well with these handsome, well-dressed people. I wandered into a bookstore, probably Brentano's, with open doors and people browsing. From a round oak table, I picked up a book on remarriage in America. It was mostly statistics, and based on my age and circumstances, the chances were less than one in a thousand. I clapped the book shut, lifted my chin, and strolled on home.

"You look great," Ali said. "And not too made up. Can I try your stuff?" She put on some lipstick, my two blushes, and did her eyes in copper shadow. I was surprised at how well she handled the makeup. It made her look older, a stunner.

That Saturday morning I got up extra early for the boards. I had to shower, blow my hair dry and apply my new makeup. That took almost an hour. As soon as I got to the right ballroom at the Hyatt

Regency near Grand Central, I saw welcoming faces. One of the professors from UC said, "You look terrific. Why haven't you been snapped up yet? What's wrong with these Eastern men?"

Five of the Examiners had taken their psychiatric residency at the Psychiatric Institute, while I was training there. We quickly agreed to a reunion lunch at a diner across the street. One of the men, Rusty Leiber, had been a year behind me. I remembered him as pudgy, hard working, and embarrassingly compliant. If he hadn't said his name, I wouldn't have known him. He was lean now with deep vertical lines in his face and had a quiet way of holding his own.

"I hoped you'd be here," he said, sitting next to me at the lunch, speaking in a low voice. "I've kept track of you. I read your papers. I knew when you got divorced and when you came back to New York."

I listened with interest as he told me about his life. He was divorced, had no children and ran a clinic in Washington, D.C., where he lived. Later he asked if we could have lunch together again on Sunday, to catch up more. I called Isabel that night and told her about him. Laughing, she wished me good luck.

I got up early Sunday morning to blow dry my hair and put my makeup on again. I wore a gray dress with a wide soft leather belt that always got me compliments.

After testing a series of candidates it was time for lunch. I walked to a small lounge inside the hotel, with frosted glass on the doors and fussy little curtains. Rusty was waiting inside, standing by a table, and wearing a khaki suit that gave him a sort of western look. He held the chair for me. The menu had a lot of fancy descriptions for plain food. We joked about it, both ordering chicken salad sandwiches on croissants. As we ate, Rusty said he came to the city often; there was so much we could do — movies, theaters, museums. Did I like to walk? Did I like walking in the Cloisters? It's going to be so much fun, he said. I relaxed, leaned back in my seat, watching him talk and smile. He had great lines in his face. *See. It can be so easy.* He told me about the movies he liked and wanted to know my favorites.

When he got up to pay the check, I sat wondering if I should have offered to split it. Women were supposed to show their independence then. If this was a business lunch, I certainly should have offered. But it seemed more like a date: he'd arranged it, he was coming on to me, and he left with the check so quickly. I put down a tip and walked to meet him. I needn't have worried so much about political correctness, because when I got to the door he said, "I did tell you I live with a woman in Washington, but she doesn't care what I do out of town."

I stepped back.

He looked at me in surprise.

I realized he didn't have a clue and burst out laughing.

That evening I was determined to let nothing get to me. I put together a dinner using Mrs. Paul's frozen fish sticks, while listening to the kids talk. Ali was going on about plans for my birthday — restaurants where we could go. She was suggesting French, Italian and Japanese. They all sounded so good. Then the kids began teasing each other. Keith had affectionate names for Ali — Botch, Big A, Ali-B-Dali. I looked at them and grinned to myself. I had such wonderful kids and such a nice apartment, with an oak fireplace and oak floor. Everything I wanted was here.

Later I called Isabel. Sitting up in bed, the blue comforter over my knees, I told her about Rusty and his Washington woman. "What these men must think of themselves," I said, laughing. She said she was sorry he turned out to be such a creep, but I said it didn't matter. I felt good, but needed a Valium get to sleep.

I woke up feeling fragile, and called my secretary to say I had a flu. Soon Isabel phoned to see how I was. When I told her I might rest up for a couple of days, she sounded worried. Her response made me feel even worse. I went to the living room, picked up Anne Tyler's *Dinner in the Homesick Restaurant*, and got so involved in it, the story of an old woman looking back at her life and how she'd done with her children, that I didn't notice the time until I heard Ali come in. She talked with me for a while, then asked me to go out shopping with her. I said yes, but when I started to get up, I felt light-headed. I tried to convince myself I was just tired. Later, still not feeling well, I couldn't get myself out for my birthday dinner.

Keith and Ali tried to make the evening festive, but I was distracted by all kinds of worries.

Early the next morning, I went to the Jefferson Market, and felt faint while standing at the meat counter. I had to admit my anxiety was back. I tried to fight it, but each day it got worse. On Wednesday I called Isabel, and asked if she knew a doctor who could help me. She recommended an analyst, a Sid Warshofsky. After making an appointment with him for Friday, my spirits lifted.

I was determined to take charge of my life again. But when I opened my apartment door the next morning, I couldn't cross the threshold. I couldn't believe what was happening to me. I tried to focus on acting normal in front of the children. I ordered food from Jefferson Market so they'd think I'd been shopping. Before they got home I went to the kitchen to begin dinner. When I heard Ali at the door, my hands started shaking. I wanted to beg Keith and Ali to stay with me, tell them how much I needed them both. I managed not to say that, but I couldn't stop myself from crying all through dinner. I'd never felt so sick. I couldn't leave the house. I couldn't function. I couldn't trust what might come out of my mouth.

Chap 25. Dr. Warshofsky

I sat huddled in the back of a cab going to see Warshofsky. I walked slowly through a lobby with black marble walls, took the elevator to the eighth floor, and inched my way down a long hall. My fingers felt numb as I rang his bell. The waiting room was small with worn leather chairs; there was a wooden table heaped with magazines and in the back an open closet with mostly empty hangers. I sat with my coat on, hands in my pockets.

A woman rushed by me and out the door. Then Warshofsky was standing before me, his large pink hand extended. I saw curly blond hairs on the backs of his fingers. He was a big, bearded man, with a tweedy green sweater covering a substantial middle. His handshake was warm, his voice pleasant. I followed him into a large office and sat on a tan leather chair. I could see in his face that he cared about me. My tension fell from me like shattered glass.

Glancing around the cluttered room, I saw a large table covered with books and journals, and a nearby stand held cups and saucers. "Thanks for fitting me in," I said, looking back at Warshofsky.

He nodded.

"It's been a terrible week." I watched his face to be sure he understood. "I was too anxious to get to work. Yesterday I couldn't even leave my apartment. Then at dinner I kept crying in front of my children." I fished a tissue from my pocket.

165

"Sounds pretty frightening." His voice had just the right mix of calm and concern.

I slipped my coat off and sat back. "I get anxious a lot, that's my problem. But my anxiety's never been like this. Something's happening to me."

"Go on." He took a pad out and opened it, but his eyes stayed on me.

I started slowly, taking him through my birthday week. He asked a few questions to clear things up. I went on about Sinai, New York, my children. I sped up as I talked about California and Michael, then hurried back to childhood, to my mother, my father, and Yollie. While I was still speaking, he said, "We have to end soon. I want to leave some time for us to talk."

I looked at my watch, surprised I'd gone on for so long. Damp tissues filled my lap.

"Are there questions you want to ask me?"

"Yes." I looked into his eyes. "Does this make any sense to you?"

He was quiet for a while, then extended his thumb. "Look, your children are leaving. Keith's going off to college, and Ali's growing up." His index finger went up next. "Your friends are marrying, so you feel left out." Middle finger. "You don't seem to like your job much." Ring finger. "You're eager to be married, but there's no man in your life."

He kept his fingers in the air, their backs facing me. I thought how funny, so I'm the person with all those problems. We made three afternoon appointments for the next week. I wanted to come after work, but he had no openings then.

In the small bathroom papered in faded blue floral, a metal shelf held Band-Aids, liquid Ivory Soap, paper towels, and disposable cups. Two thick white terrycloth towels hung on a wooden bar by the mirror. His bathroom was like his office, like him, really. Everything necessary was there, but there was no thought about style. I liked his lack of pretense. He was a nice man, and he had a feel for who I was. Walking back through the gleaming lobby, I felt hopeful, almost normal.

I spent the weekend close to home, testing myself. First, I walked up Sixth Avenue past the Balducci's windows looking at chocolate dipped strawberries, then up Tenth Street to Hudson Avenue. I strolled along Hudson to Bleeker Park where children in hooded jackets scrambled up and down yellow sliding ponds as their parents watched. I shopped in Jefferson Market, filling a red plastic basket with canned soups, broccoli, almonds, raisins and basmati rice; I wasn't ready for the meat counter yet. On Sunday I browsed in Three Lives Bookstore on Tenth and Waverly. Tracy, the woman with sleeked back white hair, said, "Nice to see you again." I felt momentarily tearful. The children were cautious with me and asked no questions. I told them I was better.

Monday I went back to work, Valium in my pockets. When my anxiety came, I told myself I'd be seeing Warshofsky soon. He wouldn't let me fail.

Heading for my two o'clock session, I walked down Madison Avenue thinking about what to say. I felt happy to see him when he opened his door, wearing a brownish green sweater and sandals over his socks. I wondered if he had foot problems.

Settling into the patient's chair, I said, "I'm back at work. I feel much better."

"Good." He put his book on his lap. "Why don't you start? You know how this works."

I talked about my weekend, then went back to where I'd stopped. When I got to Yollie, I started to cry. I stopped myself and talked slowly, picking my words with care.

"Look we've got a problem," Warshofsky said. "If you keep yourself from crying, you won't get to your feelings. You know that."

"But then at work ..."

"I know. You have to make choices."

Making the choice was easy; doing it was hard. Letting myself cry in session felt unnatural and coming back to work with swollen eyes embarrassing. But the hardest part was saying the things that popped into my head. Once, early on, I wanted to ask Warshofsky if he thought I was pretty, but couldn't get the words out. A few sessions later, he said something funny and smiled. The way he drew back his lips looked sexy. I wanted to jump up and kiss him.

"I felt something for you just then," I said.

"Can you say what?"

I shook my head no.

"Was it about wanting to be closer to me?"

"In a way."

"It's hard being a patient. Isn't it?" He smiled.

More and more, I talked about what came into my head. I said I was vicious, selfish, monstrous — I had so much good in my life, but couldn't be happy. After a while those feeling shrank, and I laughed at some of them. It was more embarrassing still to talk about feeling attractive, or smart, or important. By Thanksgiving I knew that Warshorsky could help me. He became so necessary, it was painful. I was nervous before I saw him and dressed up for my sessions. I thought about him all the time.

It was a cold winter, and darkness came early, making me feel lonelier. I talked a lot about how much better I'd feel with a man in my life. Usually Warshofsky nodded, but one afternoon, scratching under his sweater at the wrist, he said, "You know, for someone so eager to be married, you make no effort to meet men."

His words triggered my anger, "No effort. You don't understand anything. I dress up for work every day. I go to parties where I don't want to be. I take courses at the New School. You're a married man, you don't know anything about this."

"Then tell me."

I felt lots of different feelings, but mostly hurt and angry. He kept talking, trying to get me to focus on what was happening between us. I heard his words, but they didn't register. I wanted to sneak out of his office.

Back at Sinai, sitting at my desk, I felt I had to show him that men were still interested in me. He hadn't said they weren't, but that's how I took it. I wanted to prove to him, to myself, that I was attractive. I sat thinking what to do. I was attracted to Joe from Aikido. He seemed interested in me. I got the phone book, found his work number, and after a bout of nervous coughing, called him.

That night we met in a restaurant near Wall Street where Joe worked. It took two hands to keep my wineglass from shaking, but I liked sitting across from him and feeling desired. Joe looked appealing with his glossy dark hair and bright smile. We bantered a little — Good to see you. I was so surprised you called. Steaming plates of spaghetti arrived at the table. I said I'd hesitated to see him before because of the *dojo* rumors.

He smiled. "What rumors? What are they saying about me now?"

"Well, that you're having an affair with Audrey, for one thing."

"Oh that." He took a long sip of wine. "That's been going on for years. There's not much romance between us. It's really over, but I can't bring myself to end it. Is there something else?"

I was surprised at this quick admission; probably it was an open secret. I asked about his seeing other students.

He put his fork down. "Look, occasionally I've gone out with women who came to the *dojo* once, who were never coming back. And they came after me. But this — what we're doing now — I've never done this before."

I knew I was special. It felt good to have him say it.

We took the BMT, the D train, back to his apartment in Brooklyn. He lived out near Coney Island, where lit-up Christmas figures, Santa and his reindeer, stood on dried patches of lawn. I liked being there. The houses reminded me of my old neighborhood in Brooklyn before it became Hasidic and the big fences went up, before my house on Avenue L acquired lilac trim and a six-foot wall.

Joe's apartment was done with care. As I came in, I saw a Samurai sword hung in an elaborate red and gold sheath. Framed pictures of his two grown children were under the sword, and off to side was a picture of him when he made black belt. He had a maroon futon, left unfolded, and a huge TV.

We spent the evening talking and making love. I had a sense of fitting with him. We fit physically, we laughed at the same things. He said he loved me. I said I loved him too.

It was late and I was going home by car service. Before I left, Joe made scrambled eggs and toast.

"You know, I'm not so good at this romance thing. I'm not someone you can really count on." He spooned the eggs onto my plate, his mouth tense.

I was pleased to see his tension. It meant he was afraid to lose me. "We've only had one date," I said, taking what I hoped was a worldly tone. "I don't expect you to just drop everything for me."

Joe smiled and ate his breakfast. He kissed me before I left.

I was pleased. Joe looked up to me because I was a psychiatrist. I'd listened carefully when he talked about his past, and at times I'd been useful in explaining him to himself. And he did like me. We could work all the rest out. Joe called later to make plans for the weekend.

I swept into Warshofsky's office that Friday afternoon, feeling proud of myself. After all, there was now a man in my life, one I'd known for a couple of years. Why, I'd practically solved one of my biggest problems.

"I'm not sure I get this," Washofsky said. "I thought you were looking for a man who'd stand by you."

"Joe can stand by me, he loves me."

"Maybe he does, but he told you not to count on him. He knows himself."

"No, he doesn't. He's insecure, and when he feels sure of me, sure of my love, he'll change."

"And you're so sure of your love?"

"Of course."

Warshofsky was looking at me with a puzzled expression.

I felt embarrassed and thought about saying how little the difference in our backgrounds meant to me, but I knew Warshofsky didn't mean that, and it wasn't quite true. I had a vague sense that this thing with Joe would never work out, but I pushed those thoughts away. I needed Joe. I just looked at Warshofsky and smiled.

"Well, let's see what happens," he said. "But remember, this man could easily hurt you."

It did hurt when Joe went off with Audrey every other weekend. He made it clear from the beginning that we could all play if we followed his rules, rules that called for him to let Audrey down when he was ready. Rather than feel angry at Joe, I blamed Audrey. Her time was over. Why was she hanging on like that? In my sessions, I slid over my hurt. It was a familiar hurt, one I could deal with — the hurt of not getting enough. Instead, I emphasized my progress in showing Joe I loved him.

Warshofsky sat listening; he looked tired.

Joe came to pick me up on alternate weekends. Ali liked having him around the house; he told jokes, and did Aikido with her. Keith didn't seem to take the whole thing seriously. Frieda and Isabel considered it a phase and urged me to pass through it fast. My support came from Amanda, my friend from San Francisco who'd been involved with a married man for years. Amanda went to seminars at Esalin where she was taught that you could leave your situation unchanged, but find happiness by changing your attitude toward it. When Joe was with Audrey, I'd get angry and jealous. Thanks to the time difference I could talk to Amanda late into the night. The trick, she said, was to take pleasure in what you had and not ruin it by being angry about what you didn't. Of course, she added, she hadn't quite mastered that herself. I'd repeat her philosophy to Warshofsky and watch him roll his eyes.

Warshofsky asked where I got the idea that if I loved someone enough, he'd change. "You haven't experienced that," he said.

I looked at him. "You know when you're really with someone, when you're laughing or making love, and things feel like they'll go on forever. Well, that's what gives me hope. Joe feels it too. He just needs confidence to let it happen."

"Just confidence, huh?"

Showing Joe how much I loved him did not have the expected effect. In fact, it made him feel restless and boxed in. He said he was sick of being pulled between two women. Sometimes he said he wanted no women. Sometimes he said he wanted more women, different women. He talked about women who flirted with him, sent him love letters, invited him different places. When Joe said he'd be home alone in the evenings, I'd call to be sure he was there. I was ashamed of myself. Amanda thought this all sounded bad. "What does Warshofsky think?" she kept asking. He asked why I felt so sexless without a man in my bed.

When the kids went off for Christmas, I asked Joe to stay with me. He came over with a little gym bag soon after they left and told me I could have Christmas Eve and a couple of days after. Then he had to spend time with Audrey — she always got New Year's. I heard him, but thought maybe when the time came he wouldn't be able to leave me. After all, I was his true love; she was an obligation.

Joe made a big dinner for Christmas Eve. He spent the day making sauce from scratch, adding sweet sausages. The smell of simmering tomatoes, garlic, and sage made the house festive. I placed pine branches around and put a wreath on the door tied with a golden bow. I draped flickering lights over the Schefflera and made a punch with champagne, cognac and fresh pineapple slices. Some friends from Aikido came for dinner, as well as Lila and Sal Fusco, old friends of Joe's from back when he was married. They were funny and seemed concerned about Joe. We ate, drank, sang and told jokes. Sal and Joe stood with their shoulders together singing Doo Wop.

After Christmas Eve, Joe roamed around my house, wearing my red velour robe. We watched TV and made love. I was happy, until I walked into my bedroom one afternoon and saw him packing his gym bag.

Chapter 26. Joe

"But I told you I'd had to be with Audrey," Joe said. "I told you when I first came over,"

I wanted to argue but was afraid I'd push him out of my life and turn into a ridiculous old lady with rouge spots on her cheeks. Yet I didn't think most older women were ridiculous: my mother had two widowed friends in their eighties, Doris and Luna, who were actively looking for men. I cheered them on, considered them lovely. Becoming ugly and laughable was my fate. In a way, I'd felt old most of my life. But now, at nearly fifty, with men on the street looking past me, I was even more confused about what men wanted from women. Clearly looks mattered, but a woman had to be sexy too, whatever that meant. But above all, to attract and hold a man, you had to be happy. And here I was forever anxious and sad and trying to hide it.

For months, I sat in sessions wondering whether to leave Joe. I was fed up with myself. I began to realize that I hung on to him partly to keep Warshofsky at a distance. I knew Warshofsky liked me. I knew as a therapist that I liked, more than liked, most of my patients. I rooted for them and tried not to let them down. But I did let them down at times. My patients didn't keep me in San Francisco. What if Warshofsky wanted a change of cities?

Somewhere toward spring, as the leaf buds opened, my feelings for Joe changed. Sometimes, I'd look at him and know exactly what he'd look like as an old man. There were lines around his mouth, and I knew they'd bite deeper. His eyes would be bitter, and his expression would say — life passed me by. Sitting beside him while he watched his ballgames grew boring. The idea that he was keeping me alive and vital no longer made sense.

When I came to my next session I felt shy — as if my treatment was just beginning. I told Warshofsky about Joe. He was pleased and said so. I wanted to tell him I really needed him. Instead, we talked about Joe, and men, and how much I wanted a partner. In the middle of the session my heart started racing.

"I'm getting anxious," I said.

"What's happening?"

"I'm not sure." I tried to trace my thoughts back. "Well, I was picturing myself at a single's mixer."

"And that makes you anxious?"

"Sure. I'd end up standing alone with no one to talk to, feeling no one wants me."

"Isn't that your usual fantasy?"

I nodded and felt slightly better. I looked around the room thinking about my choices.

The first mixer I went to was hosted by a group called Physicians for Social Responsibility. It was on the Upper West Side in the finished basement of an apartment house. The streets were wet and shiny from the off-and-on rain that day. I went to the basement and stood outside the door. A well-dressed woman in a red raincoat, who looked even older than I was, walked in. I followed behind her. At the back of the room, tables covered by white paper, held chocolate chip cookies, cheddar cheese doodles, ruffled potato chips, and two big bowls of pink punch. About thirty women were standing before the tables, talking and snacking, and to my relief, no men. Later on I did see three or four of them, standing together. I ended up spending time with Dee, a smiling woman with big blue eyes, curly red hair and a long green jacket that masked a plump middle. She said it was usually like this with five to ten women for every man.

Dee was a therapist, a social worker, who lived near me. She'd just gotten out of a long-term relationship and was wondering if that was a mistake. She wasn't meeting men, and the whole thing was turning her into a dumpling. Dee looked about my age, maybe a little younger. I liked her, and together we went to more mixers hosted by Physicians for Social Responsibility or Educators for Social Responsibility, but these groups had almost no men.

Going to the meetings of Parents Without Partners was a different story. Almost half the singles were men looking for women, and many weren't even parents. At my second meeting, I was asked out. I'd promised myself that if a man seemed reasonable, I'd see him twice. Lucian Singer, the man who asked me out, was definitely reasonable. A biologist at Rockefeller, he was funny, had European manners, lank white hair that topped classic features, but there was something about him that disturbed me — something prissy about his mouth. We went to a nearby restaurant for coffee. As he spoke, he leaned his arm against mine. I wanted to run out, but sat smiling trying to figure out what I was feeling. Did I dislike him? Was I attracted to him and being defensive? He had my phone number, and he said he'd call. At home I felt sick to my stomach, and worse when the phone rang. He'd want to kiss or make love, but I couldn't even touch him. Yet I felt not seeing him was the kind of neurotic sin that would keep me from meeting the right man forever. Maybe he was the right man? I thought about him all the time.

I couldn't wait to see Warshofsky. As I walked in for my Monday Appointment, the doorman smiled. Warshofsky's inside door was open and he called me in. I quickly spilled out my troubles over Lucian.

"But you can't go against yourself like that," he said. "Why does your whole fate hang on this one man?"

"I don't know, but it feels like it does. Like I have to get through my anxiety with him to know what I feel about men."

"You're learning that here." Warshofsky sat forward. "And even if he was created as your soul-mate — and it doesn't sound like he was — he's not your last chance."

I relaxed. Warshofsky had let me off the hook. He seemed the only one who could do it. Soon I found myself with embarrassing sexual longings for him.

"I want to sleep with you," I weakly confessed one day.

"You want a lot of different things from me now," he said calmly. He waited to see what I'd say, but I wasn't about to go on with that one. I sat smiling and looking round the room, hoping for a neutral subject. Philip came to mind.

I reminded Warshofsky about how I'd been in love with Philip, but when he came back after his internship, grown up and ready to marry, I'd pushed him away.

"It was the biggest mistake of my life," I said. "I should have taken the strongest medicines I could to stop my panics and married him."

Warshofsky nodded. "I think we should look at what happened back then."

"I've looked and looked, and I still don't understand."

"Well, we should look again."

I talked more about Philip. I talked endlessly about Philip. I had his number in Boston. I wanted to call him. See him. He strode through my dreams, smiling and cocky. I was anxious in the streets on my way to my sessions. Would I go into a panic, and without wanting to, push Warshofsky away? And this merging of past with present, of love with terror, was taking place in the strange, slippery world of therapy, where relationships are real and not real, and you can push away someone who still stays with you.

Chapter 27. Treatment

Like many analysts Warshofsky took a vacation during all of August. As I faced my first month without him, I worried about a repeat of my birthday anxiety and said so frequently. Before leaving, he gave me his phone number in Maine, saying if I was anxious, it would be better to call him than his backup. I felt reassured and flattered. This wasn't standard procedure, but it wasn't unheard of either.

"I don't like it," Jerry said, shouting over Frieda's wheezing air conditioner. "He shouldn't single you out like that. Maybe he has some ideas he shouldn't."

"He's not like that. It's not like that between us."

"Well, you certainly talk about him enough," Jerry said, raising his eyebrows. "Are you going to tell me you don't have sexual fantasies about him?"

"Look, I do special things for some patients. So does Frieda. It doesn't mean we want something from them."

Frieda nodded, pulling a loose-knit aqua sweater around her shoulders.

"Ladies, this you don't understand. How many attractive men do each of you treat? None — right? Well, I treat children, and their mothers come parading before me, one more appealing than the next. Why before Frieda, I ..."

"You what? Screwed those women?"

Jerry sighed, shaking his head.

August went by quickly, and I didn't call Warshofsky. I'd developed what Frieda called a rhythm of living my own life. Aikido was part of it. I'd stayed away for a while because of Joe, but I'd gotten back to practicing regularly. I'd even passed another test.

I felt nervous seeing Warshofsky after such a long break, and excited too. Dressed in a new pale blue linen suit, I sat in his waiting room glancing at *The New Yorker*. He came out of his office, tan, slim, clean-shaven, and sporting a navy blazer. When I took my seat across from him, I saw that his gold ring was gone.

"Ohmigod. You're having a mid-life crisis in the middle of mine. Are you all right?"

"Yes, yes, I'm fine." He shot me his lets-begin-the-session look.

"You can't be fine. You've just separated. Haven't you?"

Warshofsky looked uncomfortable. In 1983 many therapists didn't answer personal questions.

"Look, what else could it be?" I said. "You shaved your beard. You've lost weight. You took off your ring. And you're blushing."

Warshofsky face grew redder. "You're right. I'm being silly. I did separate, but I'm fine."

I said I was sorry. I was eager to hear more, but he said nothing else about it. I talked about the summer and Keith going off to college.

When I told Isabel about Warshofsky's separation, she said that after her husband died, she sometimes burst into tears in front of her patients. When I told Jerry and Frieda, Jerry pulled off his glasses. "I told you," he said, waving his glasses at me. "I warned you. If that man has any character, he'll send you to another therapist right now."

"I don't want another therapist. I'm comfortable with him. He knows me. Just stop it."

Jerry looked like a misunderstood mother. "I'm just trying to help. Marjorie you're not smart about men. You don't need another therapist who lets you down."

I looked at Frieda, but she wore her professionally neutral smile. *Why are you doing this?* I made some rude remark to Jerry and soon left. As I headed downtown on Broadway, two women in sleeveless dresses walked before me eating ices from small white cups.

I wondered why Jerry brought up such doubts. There was no romance between me and Warshofsky. He had no hidden agenda. Unless, of course, he was two-faced. Two-faced people scared me. When Roskolnikoff looked at the innocent infant in a carriage, and the baby turned into a leering whore, I'd dropped the book. All right, it's time you faced it. Your father was two-faced. He was your protector, but often he wasn't there. Too many things overwhelmed him. When I was a teenager and got a call from camp saying one of my bunkmates had polio, my father froze. My mother took me to the doctor for a gamma globulin shot. When Ali was little in San Francisco, my father took her to the park around the corner. She sat in a sandbox and refused to come out. My father left her alone and rushed home, claiming he didn't know what to do. I acted like it was funny, but it wasn't. She was sitting there crying. How can a three-year old child overwhelm a grown man?

Then came that old nagging question. Why didn't he protect me against Yollie? He knew. He came home once when she was chasing me around the house, saying my soul would rot in hell. He asked if we were playing a game. A game? What was he thinking? I said she always talks to me like that. She hurts me. Fire her. His face went slack around the mouth; he looked old and helpless. Mostly I forgot that face, refused to see it, locked it in some bin. Was I doing that with Warshofsky? Accept it. People you trust always turn away. You've known that all your life. No, don't slip back to that. The world isn't trustworthy or not trustworthy. Some people can be trusted up to a point. You have to figure out the point. There were plenty of times your father stood by you. You know that. Warshofsky can be trusted to do his job. You know that too.

A middle aged black man in camouflage pants and shirt grinned and asked if I could spare a hundred. I laughed and gave him a dollar.

My life didn't turn a corner when I realized I could trust Warshofsky, but something eased up. I still hated single events, but if someone asked me out, I'd either go or not go, but I wasn't so frantic.

As one part of my life improved, another gave trouble. In late September, Dr. Boyer, one of the outpatient psychiatrists, told me he heard he might be laid off as part of a restructuring of outpatient. That was the first I knew of it. I rushed up to Bloch's office. His door was open, and he was on the phone. He motioned for me to sit.

I sat in a chair with curved wooden arms. Bloch smiled, and rolled his eyes at the way the person on the phone was yammering on.

After he hung up I said, "Jim Boyer just told me there are rumors about restructuring outpatient that include letting him go. What's happening?"

"Hey relax. There are no plans. You want a cup of coffee? On me."

On him — he had to feel guilty to say that. "Rumors come from somewhere. Usually from this floor. What's happening?"

"There are no plans." He cleared his throat, making a phlegmy sound. "Sternbach's under pressure. You know that. We keep talking about how to look better with less. We talk about it all the time. We talked about beefing up outpatient, maybe getting a big name in, someone in psychopharm. You'd like that, wouldn't you? We don't even know if we have enough money in the budget. Now relax. You run a good service. No one said you didn't."

I sat looking at Bloch. He looked back smiling, courteous. *Another bad sign.* "No, it's gone further than that. If I heard who'd be laid off, there's a plan. Why aren't I part of it?"

"You will be, when and if there is one."

Then I got it. "I'm not at the meetings because you may give the big shot my job. He'll run the service, if that's what he wants."

Bloch lit a cigar.

I waited.

I waited.

I left.

I sat in my office, feeling the kind of anger that made me want to go back upstairs, grab Bloch by his beard, drag him to Sternbach's office and smash his head through Sternbach's precious glass table. My fingers were rigid and shook. I thought of calling Warshofsky, but I was in control of myself. I had one more meeting, then I'd get out of the building.

I walked down Madison Avenue trying to calm down. I'd had enough of Sinai, but I didn't want to leave academia; a major turf war was going on in Psychiatry that I had a stake in.

From the beginning, anxious patients were treated by a simple either/or approach — either they got therapy or they got medications. In the sixties, psychoanalysts led psychiatry, and they taught that using medications to treat anxiety was wrong, because drugs obscured the conflicts they were trying to resolve. But in the seventies after Schizophrenia, Manic-Depression and many severe depressions were found to be genetic, and better medications appeared, biological psychiatrists began successfully challenging the analysts. Many of them claimed anxiety was caused by a chemical imbalance that could simply be corrected by medications.

By the mid-eighties, prominent analysts, like Arnold Cooper, changed their views about medicating anxious patients. He wrote that not all anxiety was caused by internal conflicts, and that chronic anxiety often had a biological as well as a psychological basis. This reversal was based on new findings: people with chronic anxiety were shown to have lowered thresholds for panic and anxiety responses because of differences in their brain functioning. Also, since we had newer, more effective drugs, many anxious patients entering therapy wanted medicine. Prozac had arrived. Like the earlier anti-depressants, it often stopped panics, but without such unpleasant side effects.

In the nineties we learned that Panic Disorder had a genetic component, but most of those studies also showed that genetics was not the main determining cause. My own work suggested that childhood maltreatment was a major factor in passing Panic across the generations. Current research backs this finding. Neglect and abuse in childhood actually changes the individual's biology in ways that make Panic Disorder more likely. Thus, childhood maltreatment has a two-pronged effect: individuals learn patterns of interacting that make anxiety more frequent, while creating biological changes that render them less able to cope with it.

Driven by psychiatric politics and economics, the pendulum appears to be swinging back to medications alone, but that would be a profound mistake. I have seen patients whose panics were well controlled by medications, but were still unhappy with their lives. Others have reported similar findings. I believe that most adults with chronic panics need help to understand and resolve the psychological problems that plague them. I'd hoped to continue studies showing the importance of psychological factors in Panic.

But as much as I wanted to stay in academia, Sinai wasn't the way to do it. I started making calls and checking the ads in New York Times. After a while, I found that two academic positions would be available in June of 1985 when my contract was up. The first was a Chairmanship of Psychiatry at Queens Hospital Center, a city hospital in Jamaica. I called the doctor who'd run the ad and felt encouraged, but the more I thought about that job the more I knew I couldn't do it. How could I be chairman if I couldn't get up on a stage to introduce people and make announcements? Isabel said that if I really wanted it, I could take behavioral training to get over my stage fright. But I didn't want to put myself through so much then. And I never wanted to be a chairman. The other position was running outpatient at Metropolitan Hospital, the city hospital right by Sinai, but their politics were also overwhelming. My academic career seemed suddenly over.

Chapter 28. Leaving Sinai

As 1985 rolled on, I worried about my next step. I had a private practice and there was a clinic near my house where I could work part time. After a bit of weighing options, I wrote a letter resigning at the end of June when my contract was up.

At first being a lame duck at Sinai got to me. I coughed nervously when I sat at my desk each morning. Rage kicked in when I saw Sternbach or Bloch acting as if nothing had happened. I was asked not to attend certain meetings, and one of my more ambitious residents asked for another supervisor who had more clout with the department. I felt hurt and unwanted and held my head high on a neck stiff as oak. But after a while I realized few people were watching and judging me. I was getting headaches for nothing.

Although I was too upset to see it for a while, my outsider status brought me free time. My interest turned to the women psychiatrists and psychologists in private practice who supervised at Sinai. I'd wanted to know many of them better, but had been too busy to call them. That winter, I became Ms. Social. I began meeting them for lunch or coffee and found it reassuring to hear their views of treatment, life, children, and men. Mostly, I sought out women who were divorced or widowed, and discovered many of them had a love life. It wasn't quite what they wanted, but they were in no hurry to settle. They were comfortable without permanent partners, but I wasn't. They wanted lovers, companions, someone to rely on, but my needs went beyond that. I needed a man to make me feel complete and to keep me from taking too many jabs at myself.

But I did begin to think that searching for a partner should yield some fun. I read the personals in *New York* magazine, ready to answer ones that sounded encouraging, but "Sixty year old non-smoker seeks true love with slim woman, thirty-five to fifty. Send picture," was not a turn on. I didn't put my own ad in because my friends who'd done it found it depressing. Then I spotted an interesting ad in which a group of women invited men to dinner. I got together with Dee and Isabel, and our ad began: "You bring the wine, we'll do the cooking." We got plenty of responses and invited three men to dinner at Isabel's upper West Side apartment on a warm, rainy December night.

Larry arrived first, a heavy-set man in a dark suit who looked around sixty. He was connected to the theater, and after handing Isabel two bottles of Alsatian Reisling, he said, "I had three meetings today, trying to get an actor friend on Carson, but it's not going to happen. They want more amateurs who do birdcalls." He was talking fast and dabbing at his forehead with a white handkerchief. Dave came next, a lawyer, who looked astonishingly like Steve McQueen. He introduced himself in a low voice, and repeated everyone's name twice to be sure he had it right. After handing Isabel a silver wrapped bottle, he sat across from Larry on the blue sectional, drinking quickly, looking like he was trying to blot out some terrible sadness. It struck me as funny to see this handsome unhappy fellow, unknowingly sitting across from three therapists who were dying to help him.

After Larry finished a story about Barbara Streisand, Dee turned to Dave and said, "I don't want to pry, but you look a little down."

"I'm sorry." Dave seemed surprised. "I don't mean to, but you know how divorces can be."

"Oh, sure," Larry agreed. "What stage is yours at?"

"Working out an agreement, maybe?" He smiled. "But why think about that with all this lovely company around."

I looked at Dave's clear blue eyes, pulled back my shoulders, and flashed my most upbeat smile.

Dave winked at me. As the group talked, his eyes kept seeking mine.

Patsy, the third of the men, arrived, complaining about traffic and holding two bottles of Chianti. His coat was soaking wet and we hung it in the bathroom. "These are usually good parties. None of that meat rack feeling," he said, rolling up his sleeves to show impressive muscles. A smile filled his round face.

When we went to the table Dave put his hand on my shoulder and guided me to the seat beside him. I was pleased with myself. As everyone chatted, Dave let his knee drift against mine. I returned the pressure. We kept this up all through a dinner that was long, good, and accompanied by lots of our guests' wine. I'd stopped drinking after the salad, but Dave kept going. By the time we got to the Angel Food cake, his face was crimson. He raised his glass with an unsteady hand and said, "I'm so glad I came tonight. Everything looks different to me now. That bitch Janice won't get a thing."

Dave's expression was vengeful. He mumbled something about being sorry to bring his problems up again. Everyone, including me, responded with words like — no problem, tough time. Slowly, his knee drifted back toward mine, but this time mine eluded his. That flash of rage was troubling. It made me lose interest in him, and I didn't spend a moment second-guessing my feelings.

As winter passed, I felt more attractive. It was 1985, and fifty was not old. In fact fifty was in. Gloria Steinem had recently celebrated hers at an enormous Waldorf-Astoria party, looking gorgeous in an ice blue gown with silver glitter on her shoulders. Radiant pictures of her appeared on magazine covers. When a reporter said she didn't look her age, she retorted, "You don't know what a fifty-year old woman looks like." She was right: Isabel, Frieda, and Dee, were attractive. At sixty, Jackie Kennedy was still a knockout. Best of all, there were attractive available men interested in meeting women their own age. Warshofsky was available, and I couldn't picture him with some kid. I'd sit across from him at our sessions wondering how he was doing. Was he meeting women? Was he looking? He was still trim in the middle.

I tried to arrange another singles dinner, but one of us was always too busy. Then in mid March, Dee changed jobs, and we only spoke by phone. The next time I saw her was by accident.

Early on a Sunday morning, I was heading toward the Bagel Buffet on Sixth Ave, a small grungy place that made the greatest bagels. The streets were empty, except for a few people walking their dogs. Dee came strolling toward me, holding hands with a bearded man, the two of them smiling into each other's faces. She called me over and introduced him as Steve, a math professor at NYU. We stood talking for a few minutes.

Dee called me later to say Steve was her old boyfriend. They'd just gotten back together and things were going well. "He thought you were cute," she added. "He wants to fix you up with one of his friends. Fred's another mathematician, but he's like Steve. He can talk to people, but he's away this semester."

After that, Dee called frequently to report how well things were going with Steve. She began talking marriage. I felt jealous, but also hopeful, maybe I'd be next?

"Maybe you will be," Isabel said over coffee. "You're not so skittish anymore."

One late afternoon in April, after I'd left Sinai for the day, the sky cracked open. It poured. I ducked into a large corner delicatessen on Eighty-Sixth and Madison. It was close to Warshofsky's office, and sometimes I went there after my sessions to unwind.

As I sat in one of the booths, waiting for my chicken soup to cool, I heard a familiar voice behind me talking about psychoanalysis. Warshofsky. Intrigued, I thrust my head back to listen. He was talking with a teenage boy who I realized from the conversation was his son. Warshofsky's mother was there too. The boy was asking long, detailed questions, like someone struggling with a term paper.

"It's not that difficult," Warshofsky said. "You see, you have two relationships with your patient. Adult to adult, that's crucial, that makes it safe. Then, without knowing it, the patient also relates more emotionally, more as a child, and he confides things he doesn't want to admit. More and more, he sees his neurotic side. We see it together." I was fascinated by what he was saying and nodding in agreement. They got up to go.

After they passed I watched them, from over the top of my menu. The boy bent over to joke with his grandmother. She beamed at her son and grandson. As Warshofsky left, his hand rested on his son's back.

I wondered where the boy lived. How often Warshofsky saw him? And how often Warshofsky saw his mother? Had she always adored him? Freud's mother had called him "mein goldener Sigi." And I felt odd too, as if it shouldn't have happened. I mused for a while on ways therapists and patients could be kept from meeting accidentally. Then two thoughts came in quick succession: no patient could possibly be as important to Warshofsky as his son, and the boy would always be at the center of his life. That was the first time I thought seriously that my treatment would eventually end. I didn't panic, but there were anxious flutters in my chest. To stop them I pressed my palms against my ribs.

At my next session I was pensive. I told Warshofsky about seeing him at the restaurant, and my reactions. As he listened I noticed how intent his eyes were, and how his cheeks curved smoothly to the strong jaw that angled back from his round chin. His face was warm and open.

"I'm never going to get all the attention I want from you, am I?" I said, needing those words between us.

"Probably not." Warshofsky looked concerned. "That must be a disappointment."

"It is. But not a surprise."

I knew we'd spend many sessions dissecting my feelings, but I didn't want to do it then. I was quiet, or made bad jokes. When I left I felt sad, and the sadness lasted weeks. I was getting to know myself, and I accepted that inside me was a big emptiness I'd always carry.

Chapter 29. All Over Again

After I left Sinai in the summer of 1985, I saw my own patients, covered for psychiatrists on vacation, gave medications to patients of psychologists or social workers I knew, and worked in a clinic on Seventeenth Street. But there were times when I wasn't busy. During them I often thought about that emptiness inside me, and it stopped scaring me as much. Unexpectedly, I had fun.

I'd rented an office on Ninth Street just up the block from my apartment, and decorating it gave me pleasure. Mom sent articles on office design and dispensed advice over the phone — use earth tones. One article said to budget yourself so you could buy at least one good piece of furniture. I decided that would be the patient's chair, a big, comfortable one that was subtly protective. I ended up with a velvety beige chair much like the one I sat in at Warshofsky's office. As the finishing touch, I brought my prayer plant from Sinai. It gave life to the room: in the evenings it made sudden rustling sounds as its folding leaves popped into new positions. I ended up liking the warm, but not too cozy, feel of my office.

At the end of August, Keith, Ali, and I visited my parents in the Adirondacks. We started in the early afternoon, and as we drove north the air grew cooler; by evening we were bundled in heavy sweaters.

Day Lilies along the narrow road to my parent's house brushed against the car, their orange petals flashing in the headlights. Mom called from the kitchen to say our dinner was waiting, and Dad came out to greet us, holding a silver colored flashlight. Mom looked tired as she fluttered around, putting butter and milk on the table. They'd already eaten, but sat with us drinking tea as we ate orange-roasted chicken, salad and baked potatoes. Keith had finished his sophomore year at Berkeley and Ali her first year at Packer, a private school in Brooklyn. They were doing well, felt happy and showed it. Mom's eyes followed their every gesture with a look of greedy pleasure. Then she'd look at me and smile.

The next morning, the kids, my dad and I hiked into town for pizza. In the afternoon, we went to the lake with my mother. The children had grown up enough to let her march them around and introduce them to her friends. I stood watching as they, knowing it made her happy, smiled, and talked with animation.

Going back to the house, the kids went ahead, and I walked with my mom. She had shortness of breath from emphysema that was getting worse, but it seemed more than that. I asked how she was.

"Not good." She pressed her lips together and shook her head. "Something's not right. I have funny cramps, and my appetite's off. As soon as I get back to Florida, I'm going to see Dr. Gupta. We're leaving here early. Before the Jewish holidays."

I listened but didn't quite take her words in. She was nearly eighty, but she was my mother, too tough for any illness.

"Ali, you've slimmed down so much," Mom kept repeating. "You're so tall and pretty." Ali squirmed but seemed pleased. Sunday afternoon Mom announced she had some things to give Ali and me, pretty things she didn't use. We sat on her white chenille bedspread as she opened an old sewing box that held round velvet pouches with zippers. From the first one she brought out a choker of graded carnelian beads interspersed with small cut crystals. "This was my mother's," she said. "She wore it for special occasions. She wore it to my wedding." She put it on Ali, fastening the square carnelian clasp in front. With the choker around her throat and her hair pulled back Ali looked different, like a young woman of my grandmother's generation. She looked at herself in the mirror over Mom's dresser, smiled, and said, "My Russian side is coming out." And it did show in her thick eyebrows and long dark eyes. Next came small diamond stud earrings which Mom handed me. "These were my mother's too," she said. "She wore them all the time. It's time you had them." I put them right on, glad to have a tangible connection to my grandma Golda.

After that came cameos, gold chain necklaces and bracelets, a small silver mesh purse, the long white gloves from Mom's wedding, narrow and soft with pearl buttons up the sides. Mom laughed, as if giving each gift made her happier, until she was almost high on giving. She told us to pack everything up and take it. We did, and left Monday morning.

Mom called three weeks later. Stomach cancer. Operable.

My parents were out when I got to their Woodland house in Florida. They'd left a note on the kitchen table saying they were buying things for the hospital. When they got back, Mom was in high spirits, her eyes too bright. That evening we went to dinner at the Sea Shanty, a restaurant with good fresh fish and baked bread brought warm to the table. Doris, a friend from way back in their Brooklyn days, came along.

I dreaded that dinner. The Doris I knew avoided unpleasantness at any cost. My dad wasn't much better: when he visited Mom during her recent hospitalizations for emphysema, he ran out quickly. And Mom was so terrified of cancer that her hands shook when she said the word.

When we got to the restaurant, I felt I was sitting with three people I no longer knew. My father worked to be upbeat, and Doris went along with my mother's good mood, joking herself at times. Mom sat relishing her fried shrimp, dipping each bite in tartar sauce. Later she asked for more fresh bread to go with her coffee. The waitress hesitated, her hand on her hip.

"I don't have the energy to argue," Mom snapped. "Get the bread or the manager this minute." It felt good to hear her say these things that usually embarrassed me. *Lily, Lily keep that mouth going. Nothing can touch you then.*

The day of the operation Dad stood in the hospital corridor staring at the doors to the operating suites. I stood with him, but took breaks to walk around and sit. We didn't talk much, but he'd catch my eye and nod. I couldn't get him to sit, but finally convinced him to come to the cafeteria for a quick lunch. Back upstairs, he stood for three more hours, a neat stocky figure in a gray windbreaker and red socks.

People kept coming through the operating room doors. Dad looked up each time. Then a tall man in green scrubs came out with a mask dangling from his neck, and smiled at him.

"Good news, "he said, removing his mask, "we got it all. There'll be some problems, two thirds of her stomach's gone, but that can be managed."

Dad thanked him, then settled into a chair by the wall and closed his eyes. When I touched his shoulder, he smiled. I asked the surgeon if I could wait in recovery to be there when my mother woke up. He pointed to some doors. A nurse led me through a room full of unconscious people to my mother's bed. Mom, also unconscious, was fighting to pull herself to one side, making the tubes in her nose and mouth dig into her flesh. Her eyes were turned to the side, so the whites bulged forward. Unbearable terror twisted her face. For an instant, I felt her cuts extend into my flesh. I put my hand over hers and started calling to her.

"Mom, Mom, Lilly, Lilly of the Valley, wake up. You're Okay." Her body began to relax and she settled slowly onto her back. Her eyes began to focus.

"Margie, what's happening?"

"It's over. You're fine. You're fine. They got it all."

"How's Oscar?"

"Good. He's resting. He stood waiting for hours."

She smiled and pressed her hand up into mine.

"I love you," I said. And I did love her in an overwhelming way. The way I'd probably loved her when I was a small child, when her survival, her happiness, was all that mattered.

Mom healed quickly, and in a few days her friends sat around her bed. Before they arrived, she sat up, and while I held her mirror, smoothed pink lipstick on her lips and rubbed some onto each cheek.

She put on a pink sweater with a pink satin ribbon around the edges. She told jokes and relished all the gossip. Dad sat toward the back, a big smile on his face. I hovered around giving out water, tissues, fruit and cookies.

Before her friends left, Mom held each by the hand and said, "I've had a good long life. I was ready to go."

After they left, she asked me to help her walk around. She was embarrassed to go with the nurses; walking made her pass gas.

I left for New York while she was still in the hospital. She was doing well, and I had to get back to work. As I flew home, a can of diet Coke in one hand, I watched the clouds pass under me like a second ocean. I was calm. I felt close to my mother. I admired her.

Chapter 30. Meeting Myself

I looked forward to seeing Warshofsky, but not with the same urgency. I had the feeling I wouldn't get much further in treatment. Psychoanalysts no longer talked of cures, but of making small but important changes, of symptoms fading, and that's what I experienced in my three plus years of treatment. I thought about ending, but wasn't quite ready for that.

My practice was growing. Frieda was sending me patients, and so were friends from Mt. Sinai and Beth Israel. Mostly I treated anxious patients, using weekly therapy and often medications. I enjoyed the work and the freedom of making my own schedule; I could watch Ali play forward in her basketball games. But when fall arrived, and I got a call from Greg Norman, asking me to work with him at Queens, I grew excited. Greg was the former head of Inpatient Psychiatry at Sinai who'd become Chairman of Psychiatry at Queens Hospital Center, the position I'd briefly considered. I told him I was interested but couldn't think about making yet another change.

About a week later, Dee called to say that Steve's friend, Fred, was back in the city, and she was giving him my number. A few days later, a pleasant voice on my answering machine invited me for coffee.

When I called back, we groped a bit for a subject, then fell into talking about Berkeley, where Fred had been teaching math and Keith was majoring in it. It became an easy conversation about this and that, and I didn't want it to end. I said I wanted to meet someplace away from my apartment because I didn't want Ali — almost fifteen — watching, or worse still Ali and her friends. Fred picked Cafe Delle Artista on Greenwich Avenue, an old Village standby, one flight up from the street.

I walked over to Greenwich on a warm, breezy day and saw a lean, athletic man, with a surprisingly innocent expression pacing outside. After the waiter seated us by the front window, Fred asked about the daughter I was hiding from.

"Not hiding exactly," I said, "but teenagers are harsh judges. You wouldn't want her watching either."

Fred laughed, softening an angular face lightly sprinkled with freckles. We talked about Keith and Ali, my marriage, his, the world of singles. He said it was confusing. I agreed.

"I was glad to hear you were a psychiatrist," he said, looking up from his coffee. "It must be fascinating work. I went into therapy when my marriage fell apart. It helped my depression. It's a complicated process. I was impressed when my dreams started to make connections I hadn't."

It was reassuring that Fred respected my work. I asked about his.

"You sure you want to hear about Lie groups? I've lost friends that way."

"Well, if it gets that bad I'll tell you." I really did want to understand, and I'd had two years of college math.

Fred took his pen from his pocket, and on a napkin, drew a picture of a cup with a handle. I followed as he sketched a series of pictures showing how the cup changed into a doughnut, but how that led to Lie groups escaped me. He told me that Lie groups were a mixture of algebra and geometry that helped us understand the hidden symmetries of the universe, like Einstein's theory of relativity. Also they allowed us to solve problems by making them simpler. "And they're beautiful," he added looking at me with intently with eyes the color of ocean water. I felt a quiver of pleasure.

We made a date for that Saturday night, and after that for the following Saturday. He made a point of telling me when I'd see him next and when he'd call. I soon learned that "I'll call tomorrow" meant I'd hear from him in one to four days. Still I got anxious when his call was a day late. Since I was hiding my anxiety from him then, I'd be bang on the phone to Amanda. She helped calm me, so I sounded breezy when he did phone. He seemed to understand my need for clarity, and I felt, he, too, wanted clear messages about where he stood with me.

I talked about him with Warshofsky who looked happy. "Now, this fellow's got his head on straight."

I left his office feeling pleased, but as I walked on Madison Avenue, something didn't feel right. This budding relationship was not something I wanted to analyze as I lived it. It was important, and I wanted to judge it on my own. Warshofsky understood. A month later we ended treatment, and I left knowing I could always come back. From time to time I missed Warshofsky. I've always felt grateful to him.

The relationship with Fred built slowly — his doing — but it felt right to me, too. I was starting to rest against him, and knew that was premature. When we talked at first, he was sometimes sad. His marriage had lasted twenty-four years and he hadn't wanted it to end, but his wife was changing her entire life. He said he'd always wanted children, but I was past that and wondered what part that played in his sadness. He was only forty-seven. It was a lot to give up. He said he didn't mind, but I felt he did.

He was fun and easy to be with. We went hiking in the mountains near New Paltz with Dee and Steve. We went to movies and dinners with Frieda and Jerry. We went sailing with the Sullivans, friends of Fred's who had a big boat in Barnegat Bay on the Jersey shore.

After coming back from a hiking trip, I told him about my anxiety. He didn't seem to understand and said getting anxious was normal. I described the week of my forty-eighth birthday. That registered.

"So what helps with this?"

"Knowing I'm not alone."

He nodded. "I don't like feeling alone either."

He read my papers on anxiety and asked some questions. Sometimes when I told him I felt anxious, he seemed puzzled, saying how poised I looked. And I suppose that after almost thirty years of practicing to look poised when I was anxious, I succeeded at times.

Meanwhile Greg Norman kept calling to fill me in on what was happening at Queens, urging me to look the place over. I drove up in early December. The hospital looked like a college campus with different size buildings spread over tree-filled grounds. Greg's office was in a brick building near the entrance. Across from it stood the former nurse's residence that now housed the Psychiatric Outpatient Department. It was a gray building fronted by the statue of a nurse four stories high.

Greg wanted me to run Psychiatric Outpatient and help get research going. He knew I'd done research on anxiety and wanted to hear more about it. When I said my next step would be to compare the childhoods of anxious patients to those of people without symptoms, he began suggesting possible control groups at Queens. He was interested in medications for anxiety and wanted to get a better idea of how Prozac worked in Panic. He filled me in on the problems at Queens. Before I left, I told him about my own anxiety and that there were things I couldn't do, like talk on stage. It was embarrassing to say it but a relief to have it in the open. Greg was interested in that, too. How was I? What was I doing about my anxiety? Working on it, I said.

I knew I'd go to Queens, the question was when. I had to reduce my private practice and decide what to do about my office. I started visiting to learn about their outpatient program. It was nothing like Mt. Sinai. Queens was a long-neglected, teaching hospital for Long Island Jewish Medical Center, and only an occasional resident rotated through. The patients were followed by dedicated, mostly foreign-born psychiatrists who had too many cases. Other problems included getting charts on time, paint on the walls, and lights in the halls. I felt I could deal with at least some of these issues, and once again planned to set up an anxiety clinic.

As I told different colleagues what I was doing, some wondered why I didn't wait for a more prestigious job. I resented hearing that and resented the people who said it. I'd felt some embarrassment about backing down the academic ladder myself, but I was more comfortable in a smaller pond.

One Saturday in April, after Fred and I had been talking about the hospital, I drove him to see it. We took the Midtown tunnel. I was feeling confident and happy as I showed him the grounds, the budding trees, the rock solid nurse with green moss on her shoulders. Going back, he said the 59th Street Bridge would be quicker. It was one of those bright spring-like days when everything seems possible. I thought — why not? At first I drove calmly, but as the bridge came in sight my heart began to pound. My hands slid on the steering wheel. As we approached the ramp I felt dizzy and slammed on the brakes. Cars honked around us. Drivers swerved out of our way, giving me the finger. Fred started to say you can't stop like that, asked if I was anxious, and if he could help. I couldn't answer. He grew quiet and gripped his seat. Suddenly I rallied, and with Fred signaling wildly, managed to turn onto a side street. I just sat there for a while, feeling nervous and ashamed. I looked over at Fred who was taking deep breaths. "It's Okay," he said, trying to smile. "But next time maybe we should stick to the tunnel." Later, he said he had a different understanding after seeing that panic.

I planned to start at Queens in July, and as the time approached I thought about going on Prozac. Partly, I was affected by what happened on the highway, but it was Greg's influence, too. I felt foolish not trying something that could possibly help me, something I gave to patients with exactly my symptoms. Still, I had mixed feelings. Even though I often took Valium, I didn't think of myself as being *on* a psychiatric medication. Again I worried that the medication would change me, but I tried it. The Prozac stopped the anxiety I'd get at the beginnings of meetings, it stopped the tickle at the back of my throat that made me feel a panic was coming, but it didn't stop my phobias. I still couldn't get up on stage or drive over bridges. And it didn't free me from unnecessary worries either. After some months, I took myself off it, because it made me feel wired and distant from myself, and went back to using Valium as needed. Much later, when the newer anti-depressants came out, I tried Zoloft. It was a Seratonin regulator like Prozac, but with fewer side effects. I stayed on it or other drugs like it, although I took breaks from them at times. They all helped me the way Prozac had, but none was a panacea. Yet, it was a comfort not to sit in meetings, a Valium between my fingers, worrying about a panic. Unlike Valium, Zoloft didn't knock me out for hours, nor did it lead to depressive feelings, as Valium often does. Also individuals with Panic are prone to depression, and I felt the Zoloft was protecting me from that as well.

After helping me to move to Queens, Fred announced it was time to meet his family. His parents and his younger twin brothers lived in Allentown where Fred grew up. We went early in the summer. His brothers, the fraternal twins Richard and Jim, were both married, with two children each. Jim was a finance professor at Lehigh, Richard, an architect, and both their wives were teachers. Fred told me that during his adolescence, his mother, a Catholic, had become extremely religious in a way that distanced her from the family. Although she'd married a Protestant herself, she was so upset when Fred and Jim married non-Catholics that she refused to go to either wedding. His father went. As we drove, Fred jokingly warned me not to get too upset if the dinner arguments appeared to get out of hand; it was his family's way. His father, Frederick Senior, and especially his Uncle Bill, were rabid Republicans, and the boys would try to set them straight.

First, we stopped at Jim's home, a big rambling three-story house with overstuffed couches, worn chairs, and a shaggy white dog under the coffee table. Jim looked like Fred only rounder. Jan, his wife, was pretty, edging on roundness too, a warm woman with short blond hair and quick blue eyes. Over wine, Jan told me that Fred's mother had taken a long time to accept her and would probably stay distant from me because I wasn't Catholic either. Her friendliness put me at ease.

At Fred's parent's house, the dinner scene was hectic. Richard, the thin twin, was serving drinks while Diane, his glamorous, dark-eyed wife, was getting food to the table. Nephews and nieces were rushing around. Fred's father, who looked like his sons, same eyes, had a bad knee and had to be helped to walk. After saying hello, Uncle Bill said, "I empty my pockets every morning to be sure no one slipped me a Roosevelt dime. Don't you think those damn Socialists are ruining the country?" Ellen, his wife, told him to stay in line or she'd turn off his pacemaker.

I was glad I'd been warned about Fred's mother. Mary was a slim woman with a worried expression who looked away when she shook my hand. I was hurt and tried to talk with her a few times. She wasn't interested, so I stopped. But I was disappointed.

As we passed the pot roast around, Uncle Bill declared, "Anyone willing to work, can make it here." No one responded. Bill repeated himself, and Richard and Jim reluctantly began to argue. Fred chipped in too, although he spent most of his time in the more general conversation. I found Fred's father especially warm, and when the evening was over, I'd had a good time.

Driving back, it was dark, and in some of the houses a single candle flickered in each window. Fred said it was a Moravian custom. We talked about his brother's solid marriages and his parent's puzzling one. Then he asked what I'd expect if I loved someone fully.

"Marriage," I said. "Anything less and I'd feel something was being withheld."

"I guess I agree," he answered. "I've just never thought much about it. I assumed I'd be married for life." He drove quietly for a while and asked if I wanted to stay in New York.

"New York or where my kids are."

"I miss California, but my job's at NYU."

After that evening, Fred was unusually quiet, like he was thinking hard about some problem. I got anxious but kept it to myself. Then one night at his apartment, he said, "I'm not sure I love you. I feel mixed up. I'm sorry."

Once home, I couldn't move. I sat on a chair in my apartment, my arms hanging dead at my sides. I don't remember thoughts, just sadness. Fred came over Sunday night to say he was sorry. He did love me. He was just scared: it was a big thing.

After that we just kept getting closer.

Keith met Fred that summer, and it went well. Fred kept some distance. Keith was already a man. He already had a father.

Ali said, "I like him, but he could be cuter."

Beaty said, "Finally. He's funny."

At the end of the summer, I took Fred up to Fourth Lake to meet my parents. I'd told my mother we would get there after dinner. She was ready with tea, coffee, cut fruit and Mandelbrot. Mom was elegant now and Katherine Hepburn thin. Her face was strong with deep vertical creases, and her dark eyes glistened with a new expression. She looked ready to enjoy herself, or ready for whatever. Over tea, she questioned Fred about his work, marriage, family, and relationship to her grandchildren. My father read the paper, but looked up at times, to make comments like math was a terrific subject: the queen of the sciences. He'd majored in it in college. Fred's long, detailed answers pleased my mother. He said his mother was Hungarian, and he'd learned to cook from her. That interested Mom and they spent time comparing Jewish and Hungarian cooking. The next day — and it took a full day including the shopping — Fred made Hungarian chicken soup with broccoli florets and spaetzle.

Ecstatic, Mom had almost two helpings. Later she took me aside, and said, "He's nice. Very nice." She seemed to want to say more, but for once words failed her. She kept smiling and squeezing my arm.

Driving home, we took the scenic route, and I thought about how I was the same, yet different. I think about that often. I'd hoped to step from my analysis reborn as a poised, outgoing woman. But even with medication I am still a worrier, someone a bit stiff with a group of new people. But I have made major changes that fulfill me. If Zoloft had been around earlier to stop my panics, I'm sure I would have had an easier life. But the medications have not really changed me. They did not teach me to trust. That came only from knowing trustworthy people.

CHAPTER NOTES AND REFERENCES.

I have included notes and/or references for chapters in which I refer to published findings, or where further comments might add clarity.

CHAPTER 6: FORCED CHOICES
Page 39. The division between psychosis and neurosis...
From Freud's time through the sixties, psychiatrists regarded psychotic and neurotic illnesses as distinct entities. Psychotics often have severe breaks with reality, while neurotics, although they may distort reality, were considered essentially bound by it.

However, in the sixties therapists began writing about highly anxious patients who initially appeared neurotic, but during treatment lost touch with reality and often went out of control. This was one of the first indications that these illnesses were not as clearly separated as was first believed.

CHAPTER 11: CLOSE SUPERVISION
Page 80. The riddle of anxiety.

The summary of Freud's view of anxiety is based one of his last papers. The summary of John Bowlby's Attachment Theory is based on one of his major books.

●Freud, Sigmund (1926). Inhibitions, Symptoms and Anxiety. *Standard Edition* 20:75-174,1959.

●Bowlby John (1973). Separation: Anxiety and Anger, Vol. 2 of *Attachment and Loss*, New York, Basic Books, Inc. 1973.

CHAPTER 13: SINGLE IN SAN FRANCISCO
Page 94. My anxiety seeped into new places.

My frequent panics in San Francisco led to difficulty crossing bridges. This is a phobia, defined as persistent, unrealistic and intense fear of an object or situation. The initial cause of my fear was a panic attack that occurred while I was driving across the Bay Bridge. Then the fear of panicking took over until just the sight of a bridge to-be-crossed made me anxious. In phobias, underlying conflicts may or may not be present. Usually phobias are cured by approaching the feared object or situation in a controlled fashion, until eventually the connection between the object and the anxiety is broken (desensitization). My practicing going over bridges in San Francisco was an attempt to desensitize myself, but since I never learned to feel truly comfortable, my phobia did not disappear.

CHAPTER 14: BETWEEN PANICS
Page 105. Tofranil.

Tofranil is one of the tricyclic antidepressants. These also include Elavil, Norpramin, and Adapin. These medications are effective in stopping panics, but often have difficult to tolerate side effects, e.g. dry mouth, palpitations, tremor, weight gain, and confusion.

CHAPTER 16: THE ALMOSTS
Page 115. It could all have been a placebo response.

A placebo response is the sense of improvement patients report when they believe their treatment, although it contains no active ingredients or activities, benefits them. It is a powerful effect: one third of any group of patients given a placebo report feeling better.

CHAPTER 27: TREATMENT

Page 181. Anxious patients were treated by an either/or approach.

Early on, treatment for anxious patients was divided between two main approaches — the psychodynamic or the biological. The analyst Arnold Cooper was one of the first to combine these methods; he suggested medication for some anxious patients as part of their treatment. Research findings led him and other analysts to conclude that panics sometimes had a biological component.

- Cooper, AM. Will Neurobiology Influence Psychoanalysis? *Am J Psychiatry* 142:1395-1402,1985.

Page 181. We had effective new drugs.

Prozac was the first of the next generation of anti-depressants, the Selective Serotonin Reuptake Inhibitors, (the SSRIs). These include Luvox, Zoloft, Paxil, Celexa, and Lexapro. Serotonin is one of the main neurotransmitters in the brain. When it is low many individuals feel anxious and depressed. The SSRIs raise the Serotonin level by slowing its rate of re-absorption. They are effective against panics, and have easier to tolerate side effects than the tricyclics.

Page 181. The genetic versus psychological roots of Panic Disorder.

Evidence suggested that although panic has a genetic basis, genetics is not its main determining cause. My own work suggests that childhood abuse and emotion neglect are causal factors in Panic Disorder. Later it became clear that childhood abuse, in addition to its psychological effects, produces lasting biological changes that interfere with the individual's ability to cope with stress.

- Hettema JM, Neale MC, Kendler, KS. A Review and Meta-Analysis of the Genetic Epidemiology of Anxiety Disorders. *Am J Psychiatry*, 158:1568-78. 2001.
- Raskin M, Peeke HV, Dickman W, Pinsker H. Panic and Generalized Anxiety Disorder. Developmental Antecedents and Precipitants. Arch *of General Psychiatry*, 39:687-9, 1981.
- Heim C, Newport J, Bonsall RM, Andrew H and Nemeroff CB. Altered Pituitary-Adrenal Axis Responses to Provocative Challenge Tests in Adult Survivors of Childhood Abuse. *Am J Psychiatry* 158: 575-581, April 2001.

Page 182. Biological versus psychological treatment of panic.

Recent reports show that even after panics are stopped by behavioral therapy, the individual often still feels unhappy about himself and his life.

●Fava GA, Rafanelli C, Ottolini F, Ruini C, Cazzaro M, Grandi S. Psychological Well-Being and Residual Symptoms in Remitted Patients with Panic Disorder and Agoraphobia. *J Affect Disorder* 65: 185-190.

CHAPTER 30. MEETING MYSELF

Page 197. Treatment of phobias.

Although most SSRIs are effective against Panic Disorder, they are often not effective in treating established phobias, and desensitization is required.

Page 198. Panic predisposes individuals to depression.

●Wittchen HU, Kessler RC, Pfister H, Lieb M. Why do People with Anxiety Disorders become Depressed? *A Prospective-Longitudinal Community Study*. 406:14-23, 2000.